T. Lobsang Rampa

FEEDING THE FLAME

March 19- 1999
" The Journey"
" Jump from the
Mountain "
 # Cereillie, New Mexico

INNER LIGHT PUB.

FEEDING THE FLAME
T. Lobsang Rampa

Other books by T. Lobsang Rampa

THE THIRD EYE
DOCTOR FROM LHASA
THE RAMPA STORY
THE CAVE OF THE ANCIENTS
LIVING WITH THE LAMA
YOU FOREVER
WISDOM OF THE ANCIENTS
THE SAFFRON ROBE
CHAPTERS OF LIFE
THE HERMIT
FEEDING THE FLAME
THE THIRTEENTH CANDLE
CANDLELIGHT
AS IT WAS
TWILIGHT
I BELIEVE
THREE LIVES
BEYOND THE TENTH

Dedicated to:

> *Cleopatra, the most*
> *intelligent person I*
> *have ever met*
> > *and*
> *Tadalinka, the most*
> *clairvoyant and*
> *telephathic.*

These Little Girl Siamese Cats have shown
great understanding and sympathy.

Don't ever say 'dumb animals' to me. These
are intelligent, civilized PEOPLE!

> *The truest of the true.*

FEEDING THE FLAME

It saves a lot of letters if I tell you why I have a certain title; it is said, 'It is better to light a candle than to curse the darkness.'

In my first ten books I have tried to light a candle, or possibly two. In this, the eleventh book, I am trying to Feed the Flame.

RACE OF TAN

Copper is this man,
A man of daytime white,
Yellow is that man,
And one of dark night...
The four main colours,
All known as Man,
Tomorrow's unity will come
Forming the Race of Tan.

Poem by W. A. de Munnik of
           Edmonton, Alberta.

CHAPTER ONE

The more you know the more
you have to learn.

THE letter was short, sharp, and very much to the point. 'Sir,' it said, 'why do you waste so much paper in your books; who likes to read these pretty-pretty descriptions of Tibet? Tell us instead how to win the Irish Sweepstake.' The second one followed the theme very well. 'Dear Dr. Rampa,' wrote this brash young person, 'Why do you waste so much time writing about the NEXT life? Why not tell us how to make money in this one? I want to know how to make money now. I want to know how to make girls do what I want now. Never mind the next life, I'm still trying to live this one.'

The Old Man put down the letter and sat back shaking his head sadly. 'I can write only in my own way,' he said, 'I am writing TRUTH, not fiction, so . . .'

Fog lay heavy on the river. Trailing tendrils swirled and billowed, redolent of sewage and garlic it swept yellow feelers like a living creature seeking entry to any habitation. From the invisible water came the urgent hoot of a tug, followed by furious yells in the French-Canadian patois. Overhead a dark red sun struggled to pierce the odorous gloom. The Old Man sitting in his wheelchair peered disgustedly around at the clammy building. Water dripped mournfully from some mouldering concrete wall. A vagrant breeze added a new dimension to the world of smells conjured up by the fog – decaying fish-heads. *'Pah!'* muttered the Old Man, 'What a crummy dump!' With that profound thought, he propelled his chair back into the apartment and hastily closed the door.

The letter thumped through the letter-box. The Old Man opened it and snorted. 'No water tonight,' he said, 'no heat either.' Then, as an after-thought, 'and it says that for some hours there will be no electricity because some pipe or something has burst.'

'Write another book' said the People on the Other Side of Life. So the Old Man and Family Old Man went off in search of quiet. Quiet? Blaring radios, rumbling hi-fi's, and yowling children shrieking through the place. Quiet? Gaping sight-seers peering in through windows, banging on doors, demanding answers to stupid questions.

A dump where quiet is not, a pad where nothing is done without immense effort. A pipe leaks, one reports it. Much later a plumber arrives to see it himself. He reports it to his superior, the Building Superintendent. HE comes to see it before reporting it to 'the Office'. 'The Office' reports it to his Superior. He gets on the telephone, a conference is held. Much later a decision is reached. Back it comes from 'Montreal Office' to the Superior who tells the Building Superintendent who tells the plumber who tells the tenant that 'Next week, if we have time, we will do it.'

'A crummy dump' is how one person described it. The Old Man had no such delicate way of describing the place. Actions speak louder than words; long before his tenancy expired the Old Man and Family left, before they died in such squalid surroundings. With joy they returned to the City of Saint John and there, because of the strains and stresses in Montreal, the Old Man's condition rapidly worsened until, very late at night, there was an urgent call for an ambulance, hospital . . .

The gentle snow came sliding down like thoughts falling from the heavens. A light dusting of white gave the illusion of frosting on a Christmas cake. Outside, the stained glass window of the cathedral gleamed through the darkness and shed vivid greens and reds and yellows on the falling snow. Faintly came the sounds of the organ and the sonorous chant of human voices. Louder, from right beneath the window, came the music of a tomcat ardently singing of his love.

The hiss of braking tyres on the snow-clad road, the metallic clang of car doors slamming and the shuffle of over-shoe-clad feet. A fresh congregation filing in to the evening service. Muttered greetings as old friends met, and passed. The solitary tolling of a tenor bell exhorting the tardy to hurry. Silence save for the muted buzz of distant traffic in the city. Silence save for the amorous tomcat singing his song, pausing for a reply, and commencing all over again.

Through a broken pane of the cathedral window, smashed by a teen-age vandal, came a glimpse of the robed priest in solemn procession, followed by swaying, jostling choir boys singing and giggling at the same time. The sound of the organ swelled and diminished. Soon came the drone of a solitary voice intoning ancient prayers, the rumble of the organ and again a glimpse of robed figures returning to the vestry.

Soon there came the sound of many footsteps and the slamming of car doors. The sharp bark as engines coughed into life, the grating of gears and the whirring of wheels as the cathedral traffic moved off for another night. In the great building lights flicked off one by one until at last there was only the pale moonlight shining down from a cloudless sky. The snow had ceased, the congregation had gone, and even the anxious tomcat had wandered off on the eternal quest.

In the Hospital facing on to the cathedral, the night staff were just coming on duty. At the Nurses' Station, just facing the elevators, a lone Intern was giving last-minute instructions about the treatment of a very sick patient. Nurses were checking their trays of drugs and pills. Sisters were writing up their Reports, and a flustered Male Orderly was explaining that he was late on duty through being stopped for speeding by a policeman.

Gradually the Hospital settled down for the night. 'No Breakfast' signs were fixed on the beds of patients due for operations the next day. Main lights were extinguished and white-clad attendants moved to a screened bed. Silently a wheeled stretcher was moved behind the screens. Almost inaudible grunts and muttered instructions, and a still figure entirely covered by a sheet was pushed into sight. On whispering wheels the burden was carefully moved into the corridor. Silent attendants stood while the summoned elevator slid to a stop, then, as if controlled by a single thought, the two men moved in unison to propel the laden wheeled stretcher into the elevator and so down to the basement mortuary and the great refrigerator standing like an immense filing cabinet, the repository of so many bodies.

The hours dragged by as each reluctant minute seemed loathe to give up its brief tenure of life. Here a patient breathed in stertorous gasps, there another tossed and moaned in pain. From a side cubicle came the cracked voice of an aged man calling incessantly for his wife. The faint squeak of rubber soles on stone flooring, the rustle of starched cloth, the clink of metal against glass, and the moaning voice ceased and soon was replaced by snores rising and falling on the night air.

Outside the urgent siren of a fire engine caused many a sleepless patient to wonder briefly 'where it was' before lapsing again into introspection and fear for the future. Through the slightly open window came the raucous sound of a late reveller being heartily sick on the flagstones. A muttered curse as someone shouted at him, and a string of Hail Mary's as the alcohol fumes made him retch again.

The Angel of Death went about His merciful mission, bringing ease to a tortured sufferer, ending at last the useless struggle of one ravaged beyond hope by cancer. The stertorous gasps ceased, there was the quick, painless reflex twitch as a soul left a body, and the attendants with their whisper-wheeled stretcher moved forward again, and, later, yet again. He, the last one was a man noted in politics. On the morrow the yellow press would dig in their files and come up with the usual inaccuracies and downright lies – as ever.

In a room looking out over the cathedral close, and from whence a sparkling glimpse could be obtained of the sea in Courtenay Bay, the old Buddhist lay inert, awake, in pain. Thinking, thinking of many things. A faint smile flickered on his lips and was as quickly gone at the thought of an incident early in the day. A nun had entered his room, a nun more holy-looking than usual. She looked sadly at the old Buddhist and a tear glistened in the corner of each eye. Sadly she looked and turned away. 'What is the matter, Sister?' queried the old Buddhist, 'You look very sad.'

She shrugged her shoulders and exclaimed, 'Oh! It *is* sad, you will go straight to Hell!' The old Buddhist felt his mouth drop open in amazement. 'Go straight to Hell?' he said, wonderingly. 'Why '

'Because you are a Buddhist, only Catholics go to Heaven. Other Christians go to Purgatory, Buddhists and other heathens go straight to Hell. Oh! Such a nice old man as you going straight to Hell, it is *so* sad!' Hastily she fled the room, leaving an amazed old Buddhist behind to puzzle it out.

The Angel of Death moved on, moved into the room and stood looking down at the old Buddhist. The Old Man stared back. 'Release at last, eh?' he asked. 'About time too. I thought you would never come.'

Gently the Angel of Death raised His right hand and was about to lay it on the head of the Old Man. Suddenly the very air of the room crackled and a Golden Figure appeared in the blue gloom of the midnight shadows. The Angel stayed his hand at a gesture from the Visitor. 'No, no, the time is not yet!' exclaimed a well-loved voice. 'There is more to be done before you come Home.'

The Old Man sighed. Even the sight of the Lama Mingyar Dondup could not console him for a further prolongation of his stay upon Earth, an Earth which had treated him so badly through hatred fostered and encouraged by the perverted press. The Lama Mingyar Dondup turned to the Old Man and explained, 'There is yet another book to be written, more knowledge to be passed on.

And a little task connected with auras and photography. Just a little longer.'

The Old Man groaned aloud. So much always to do, so few to do it, such a chronic shortage of money – and how could one purchase equipment without money?

The Lama Mingyar Dondup stood beside the hospital bed. He and the Angel of Death looked at each other and much telepathic information was passed. The Angel nodded his head and slowly withdrew and passed on to continue elsewhere the work of mercy, terminating suffering, setting free immortal souls imprisoned in the clay of the flesh body.

For a moment in that small hospital room there was no sound. Outside there were the usual night noises, a stray dog prowling about the garbage bins, an ambulance drawing in to the Emergency Entrance of the hospital.

'Lobsang,' the Lama Mingyar Dondup looked down at the Old Man lying there in pain upon the hospital bed. 'Lobsang,' he said again, 'in your next book we want you to make it very clear that when you leave this Earth you will not be communicating with back street Mediums, nor guiding those who advertise in the cult magazines.'

'Whatever do you mean, Honourable Guide?' said the Old Man. 'I am not cooperating with any Mediums or cult magazines. I never read the things myself.'

'No, Lobsang, we know you do not, that is why I am telling you this. If you had been reading those magazines we should not have had to tell you, but there are certain unscrupulous people who advertise consultative services, etc., and pretend that they are in touch with those who have passed over. They are pretending that they are getting advice and healing and all that from beyond this Earth which, of course, is utterly ridiculous. We want to make it very clear that you are not in any way encouraging that trickery or quackery.'

The Old Man sighed with some considerable exasperation and replied, 'No, I never read any of those magazines, neither English nor American. I consider they do more harm than good. They accept misleading advertising, and much of it is dangerous, and they have such personal bias and such personal dislike of anyone not in their own little clique that they actually harm what they pretend they are helping. So I will do as you say, I will make clear that when I leave this Earth I shall not return.'

Reader, Oh, you most discerning of people, may I have your attention for a moment? In fulfilment of my promise I want to say this: I, Tuesday Lobsang Rampa, do hereby solemnly and irrevocably state that I shall not return to this Earth and act as a consultant for anyone who claims that I am so acting, nor shall I appear at any mediumistic group. I have other work to do, I shall not have time to play about with these things which I personally dislike. So, Reader, if you see any advertisement at any time which purports to imply that such-and-such a person is in spiritual contact with Lobsang Rampa, call the Police, call the Post Office authorities and have the person arrested for fraud, for trying to use the mails, etc., for fraudulent purposes. I, when I have finished with this Earth in this life, am moving on a long, long way. So there it is, I have delivered that special message.

Back in the green-tinted hospital room with a window looking out over the cathedral and with its glimpse of the waters in Courtenay Bay, the Lama Mingyar Dondup was stating what was required.

'This, your eleventh book,' said the Lama, 'should give answers to many of the questions you have received, questions which are just and reasonable. You have lit the flame of knowledge, and now in this book you need to feed the flame that it may get a hold on peoples' minds and spread.' He looked grave and quite a bit sorrowful as he went on, 'I know you suffer greatly. I know that you will be discharged from this hospital as incurable, as inoperable, and with little time to live, but you still have time to do one or two tasks which have been neglected by others.'

The Old Man listened carefully, thinking how unfair it was that some people should have all the health and all the money, they could do anything and get on with their own tasks in the easiest conditions possible, whereas he had suffering, continuous persecution and hatred from the press, and shortage of money. He thought how sad it was that there was no Medicare in this Province and how expensive medical bills were.

For some time the two, the Old Man and the Lama Mingyar Dondup, talked as old friends will, talked of the past, laughed over many incidents which were not funny at the time they occurred but were most amusing in retrospect.

Then at last there was a shuffling of footsteps as a night orderly went about his duties. The Lama Mingyar Dondup bade a hasty farewell and the golden light faded, and the bare hospital room was once again in the blue gloom of early morning.

The door was pushed open and a white-clad orderly just moved in with his flashlight forming a pool of light round about his feet. He listened to the sound of breathing, and then quietly withdrew and went on about his rounds. From across the corridor came the uproar and cries as the aged man incessantly called for his wife. Another voice farther down the corridor broke in with a torrent of Ave Maria's endlessly repeated, monotonously repeated, reminding the Old Man of some of the almost mindless monks who repeated Om Mani Padme Hum incessantly without a thought as to what it actually meant.

From somewhere far away a clock struck the hours, one, two, three. The Old Man tossed restlessly, the pain was acute and made more acute by the strain through which he had just gone. On the day before he had had a total collapse, and even in a hospital a total collapse is a matter of some concern. Three o'clock. The night was long. From somewhere out in the Bay of Fundy a tug boat hooted as it and some others went out to bring in an oil ship waiting to berth by the oil refinery.

A shooting star hurtled across the heavens leaving a glowing trail behind it. From the cathedral tower an owl hooted, and then, as if suddenly ashamed of the noise he was making, emitted a squawk of fright and flapped off across the city.

Four o'clock and the night was dark. There was no moon now, but suddenly the shaft of a searchlight wavered across the Bay and came to rest on a small fishing boat which probably was fishing for lobsters. The light snapped off and into sight came a tug towing a very large oil ship. Slowly they ploughed through the turgid waters of Courtenay Bay, slowly the bright red light on the port side of the oil ship came into view and moved across the field of vision, to be hidden behind the Old Peoples' Home standing close.

Outside in the corridor there was sudden hushed commotion, whispering voices, the sound of controlled hurry. Then a new voice, an Intern hurriedly roused from his bed. Yes, an emergency and the need for an immediate operation. Quickly the orderly on duty and a nurse got the patient on to the wheeled stretcher, quickly it was hustled past the doors and down in the elevator to the operating area two floors below. For some minutes there were whispering voices and the rustling of starched clothes. Then all noise stopped again.

Five o'clock. The Old Man started. Someone was standing beside him, a white-clad orderly. Brightly he said, 'I just thought I'd tell you there's no breakfast for you this morning. Nothing to drink either.' Smiling to himself he turned and walked out of the room. The Old Man lay there marvelling at the crass idiotic stupidity which made it necessary to awaken a patient who had just gone to sleep, awaken him that he could be told there was no breakfast for him!

One of the most frustrating things is lying in a hospital bed, hungry and thirsty, and having just outside one's open door an immense contraption stuffed with food – ready pre-pared breakfasts for every patient who could have breakfast on that particular floor. But the Old Man glanced to his right and there it was, 'No Breakfast', plain as could be. He stretched out his hand for a drink of water, but – no, no water either. Nothing to eat, nothing to drink. Others were having their breakfast; there was a clatter of dishes and the noise of trays being dropped and slammed around. Eventu-ally the turmoil ceased and the hospital was setting about its ordinary morning business, people to go to the Theatre, where they wouldn't see a good show either, people to go to X-ray, people to go to Pathology, and the lucky ones to go home. Perhaps the luckiest ones of all were those who had passed over to one's 'true Home.'

The Old Man lay back in his bed and thought of the pleasures of passing over. The only difficulty is that when one is dying it is usually the physical breakdown of some part – some portion of one's anatomy has been invaded by a dread disease, for instance, or something is being poisoned. Naturally, that causes pain. But dying itself is painless, there is nothing to fear in dying. As one is about to die there comes an inner peace, one gets a sense of satisfaction knowing that at last the long day has ended, work has ceased, one's task has either been done, or, for the time being it is being sus-pended. One has the knowledge that one is 'going Home.' Going Home to where one's capacities will be assessed and where one's spiritual health will be built up.

It's a pleasant sensation really. One is ill, one is in the last stages, pain suddenly ceases to be acute and there is a numb-ness followed quite speedily by a feeling of well-being, a feeling of euphoria. Then one becomes aware that the physical world is dimming and the astral world is brighten-ing. It is like looking at a television screen in the darkness; the picture is darkening, there is nothing to distract from the picture on the television screen if everything else is in dark-ness. That television screen represents the life on Earth, but let the dawn come, let the rays of the sun come shining in the window to impinge on the television screen, and the brightness of the sun will make the television picture disappear from our sight. The sunlight represents the astral day.

So the physical world which we term 'Earth' fades away. People look faint, their images look faint, they look like shadows, and the colours of the Earth disappear and the Earth becomes peopled with grey phantoms. The sky, even on the brightest day, turns purple, and as one's sight on the Earth fades one's sight in the astral brightens. About the deathbed we see helpers, kind people, those who are going to help us to be reborn into the astral world. We had attention when we were born into the world which we call Earth, perhaps a doctor, perhaps a midwife, perhaps even a taxi driver. No matter who, it was someone to help. But waiting for us to deliver us on to the Other Side are highly experienced people, highly trained people, people who are completely understanding, completely sympathetic.

On Earth we have had a hard time, a shocking time. Earth is Hell, you know. We have to go to 'Hell' for all sorts of things. A lot of children think school is Hell too. Earth is the school of wayward humans. So, we are in a shaken condition, and most people fear death, they fear the pain, they fear the mystery, they fear because they do not know what is to happen. They fear they are going to face some wrathful God who will stick a hay-fork into some part of their anatomy and toss them straight down to old Satan who will have the branding irons all ready.

But all that is rubbish. There is no such thing as a wrathful God. If we are to love God then we have to love a kind and understanding God. Talk of fearing God is nonsense, it is criminal. Why should we fear one who loves us? Do you fear a really kind and understanding father? Do you fear a really kind and understanding mother? Not if you are sane. Then why fear God? There is a God, very definitely there *is* a God, a kind God. But, back to our deathbed.

The body is upon the bed, the sight has just failed. Perhaps the breath is still struggling in the chest. At last that too fades, ceases, and becomes no more. There is a twitch which journalists would probably call a convulsive shudder of agony. It's nothing of the kind. It's painless, or, to be more accurate, it is a pleasurable sensation. It's like shrugging out of a cold and clammy suit of clothes and being able to get the warm air and sunlight on one's body. There is this convulsive jerk, and then the astral body soars upwards. The feeling is indescribable. Can one imagine what it is like to be swimming in champagne with all the little bubbles bounding against one's body? What is the most pleasurable holiday you have had? Have you been on the sands somewhere, just lazing away with the sunlight pouring upon you and the sounds of the waves in your ears, and a gentle scented breeze ruffling your hair? Well, that's crude, that's nothing compared to the reality. There is nothing which can describe the pure ecstasy of leaving the body and 'going Home'.

The Old Man thought of these things, delved back in his memories, and knowing what was and what was to be, the day was passed, the day was endured would perhaps be a better statement, and soon night came again. In this hospital there were no visitors, no visitors at all. An epidemic in the whole area had caused all the hospitals to be closed to visitors, so patients were on their own. Those in public wards could talk to each other. Those who were in rooms alone, stayed alone – and it was jolly good for meditation, too!

At last, a day or two later – it seemed an eternity – the Old Man was sent home. Nothing could be done, no cure, no operation, no hope. And so he decided to do as requested by those knowledgeable people on the Other Side of life, write the eleventh book. And it is going to be answering people's questions.

For several months past the Old Man had been carefully combing the forty or so letters which arrived every day, and picking out those which had questions which seemed to be of most general interest. He wrote to a number of people in different countries suggesting that they should do a list of questions they wanted answered, and some very good friends were made. We must not forget our old friend, Mrs. Valeria Sorock, but the Old Man wants to thank in particular these for providing questions which will be answered in this book:

Mrs. and Miss Newman.
Mr. and Mrs. 'Yeti' Thompson.
Mr. de Munnik.
Mrs. Rodehaver.
Mrs. Ruby Simmons.
Miss Betty Jcssee.
Mr. Gray Bergin.
Mr and Mrs. Hanns Czermak.
Mr. James Dodd.
Mrs. Pien.
Mrs. Van Ash.
Mr. John Henderson.
Mrs. Lilias Cuthbert.
Mr. David O'Connor.
The Worstmann Ladies.

So the Old Man was sent home. 'Sent home.' Simple little words, probably it means nothing to the average person, but to one who has never had a home until fairly recently, until fairly late in life, it means quite a thing. 'Sent home' – well, it means being with loved ones in familiar surroundings where sorrows are not so great, sorrows shared are sorrows halved or quartered. So, the Old Man was sent home. Miss Cleopatra and Miss Tadalinka were there with their most serious manners to see what sort of strange creature came back from the hospital. There was much wrinkling of noses, much hard sniffing. Hospital smells are strange smells, and how was it that the Old Man was still in one piece instead of having lumps cut off? He still had two arms and legs, of course he hadn't a tail but he didn't have one before. So Miss Cleopatra and Miss Tadalinka inspected him most gravely and then came to a decision. 'I know,' said

21

Miss Cleopatra, 'I know exactly what has happened. He has come back to finish the book "Feeding the Flame" before he is taken off to feed the flame at the local crematorium. That's going to come as sure as eggs is eggs.'

Miss Tadalinka looked very grave indeed, 'Yes,' she said, 'but if he loses any more weight there won't be anything with which to feed the flames. I think they must have starved him. I wonder if we should give him some of our food.'

Miss Cleopatra jumped on the Old Man's chest and sniffed around, sniffed his beard, sniffed his ears, and had a good sniff of his mouth. 'I think he's underfed, Tad,' she said. 'I think we shall have to have a word with Ma to get him stuffed up a bit with food to fill out all those hollows.'

But no matter what Miss Cleopatra said, no matter what Miss Tadlinka said, no matter how good Ma's intentions, the Old Man was on a diet for the rest of his life, a miserable, horrifying diet, hardly enough to keep body and soul together.

Miss Tadalinka rushed under the bed to Miss Cleopatra, 'Say Clee,' she yelled, 'you know something? I've just heard them talking, he's losing a pound a day, so that means that in two hundred and seventy days he won't weigh anything at all.'

Both cats sat there thinking about it, and then Miss Cleopatra nodded her head very wisely, with all the wisdom and sagacity which comes to a Little Girl Cat four years of age.

'Ah yes,' she exclaimed, 'but you've forgotten one thing, Taddy. The hungrier he is, the sicker he is, the more clairvoyant he becomes. Soon he'll be seeing things before it happens.'

'Phooey to that!' said Miss Tadalinka, 'he does already. Look at the telepathic messages he sent us from the hospital. Still, it's good preparation for the start of his book. I think we'd better help him all we can.'

The radiator was quite warm and both little cats jumped

up to the sill above the radiators. There they stretched out full length, head to tail, and went into the usual state of introspection before communicating all the thoughts of the day to the local cats. The Old Man? Well, the Old Man was glad to get in bed. He lay back for a time and thought, 'This wretched book, suppose I have to write it. I have to live and even if I don't eat much nowadays I have to pay for what I do eat.' So, on the morrow, he decided, let's start this book with the hope that it would be finished, and here it is. It's started, you are reading the first chapter, aren't you?

Quite a lot of people have written asking things, asking all manner of questions. Well, it would be a good idea if this book were devoted to answering what appear to be common questions. People have a right to know, otherwise they get weird ideas such as those who think that death is a terrible thing, such as those who think there is no after-life. Well, it always amuses me when people say there is no after-life just because they don't know about it. In the same way a person living in a remote country area can say there is no London, no New York, no Buenos Aires because they haven't actually seen it. After all, pictures can be faked, I have seen a lot of faked pictures about life on the Other Side, and that is quite a pity. There is a very, very good 'Other Side', and it is the depth of absurdity when crooks and perverted 'seers' produce a lot of faked stuff. It's so easy to produce the actual reality, easier in fact.

I had hoped to get on with the aura research. Unfortunately I have had to leave it through lack of money, and now – well – there is no medical health scheme here, not like in England, and everything is frightfully expensive. So the aura work will have to be left for others.

There is another project which I wanted to develop and it is this: it is absolutely possible to make a device which will enable one to 'telephone' the astral world. It has actually been done, but the man who did it had such a barrage of doubts, suspicions, and accusations from the press that he got tired of it, he lost heart, and driven by the insane press he smashed his apparatus and committed suicide.

It is quite possible to make a telephone with which to telephone the astral world. Consider speech now; when we speak we cause a vibration which imparts its energy to a column of air, which in turn energizes some receiving apparatus, for example, someone's ear, and so they hear the sounds we make. It is interpreted as speech. No one has ever yet succeeded in standing atop a radio mast and shouting to the world, and being heard all over the world. For that the vibrations are transformed into a different form of energy and messages spoken and transformed into this energy can be heard, with suitable apparatus, all over the world. I listen to England, Japan, Australia, Germany – everywhere. I have even heard little America in the South Antarctic.

A device to telephone the astral is something like that. It transforms present day radio waves into something incomparably higher just as radio waves in turn are very much higher in frequency than is speech.

In days to come people will be able to telephone those who have newly passed over in much the same way as a person can now telephone a hospital and, if he is lucky and the nurse is feeling good tempered, can speak to a patient who is recovering from an operation. So it will be that those who have newly passed over and are recuperating from the strain of passing over, just as a mother and baby recuperate from birth strains, so while this recuperation process is taking place relatives can telephone a reception area and find out 'how the patient is doing'. Naturally, when 'the patient' is quite recovered and has gone to yet other dimensions he or she will be too busy to be bothered by the petty little affairs of this Earth.

This Earth is just a speck of dust existing for the twinkle of an eye in what is the real time.

For those who are interested, I have actually seen such a telephone and actually seen it in use. It's a pity that the idiot press is not subject to censorship because they should not be permitted to take foolish actions just for the sake of sensation, and so inhibit what are real developments.

So now let us consider this as a start, and the ending of the first chapter. We will go on together and see what we can do to answer some questions in the second.

CHAPTER TWO

Never reply to criticism;
to do so is to weaken your case.

THE Old Man was alone at home. Ma, Buttercup, Miss Cleopatra and Miss Tradalinka were out about the ordinary business which seems to surround all households, out shopping, because even in the best ordered communities there is always the inevitable shopping. Potatoes, soap flakes, various other things including – well, let us whisper it – unmentionable requisites without which in modern days we cannot easily manage. So the Old Man was lying back in his bed listening to the radio.

Reception was good. The programme was coming along on the African Service of the B.B.C. very clearly and with good volume. Someone was playing the new musical hits. The Old Man smiled at one piece with the unlikely title of 'Astral Journey'. He had to stop his programme because the telephone was ringing, the telephone beside his bed.

With that disposed of, he switched on again in time to hear one of the latest hits. An announcer of the B.B.C., or disc jockey, or whatever he was, announced in a decidedly Cockney voice that he was just going to put on the latest record, 'Without the Night There Would be no Sunshine'.

Without the night there would be no sunshine. Did the fellow know that he uttered a great truth there? One has to have extremes in order to have anything. Sometimes from the U.S.A., particularly on a Sunday, there comes by way of the short waves a horrible programme sent out by some gang of revivalist missionaries. The uproar, the ranting, is enough to turn anyone against Christianity. And then from a Station in South America just by the Equator there is another religious revival gang, they fairly hoot about the terrors of not being a Christian. Everyone not a Christian according to this Station, is damned and will go to Hell. Surely not the way to conduct a sane religion.

Without the night there can be no sunshine; without evil there can be no good; without Satan there can be no God; without cold there can be no heat. Without extremes, how can there be anything? If there were no extremes there would be only a static condition. Think of when you breathe, you force out your breath, that is one extreme because to all practical purposes you have no breath within you and you are in danger of suffocating. Then you take in breath and you have a lot of air in you, and if you take in too much breath too quickly you are in danger through hyperventilation. But again, if you do not breathe out and you do not breathe in, then you have nothing and you can't live.

Some remarkably foolish person in Nova Scotia sent me a silly, badly duplicated, purplish effusion about sinners and Satan. Apparently the idea was that I should send them some money as that would help wipe out Satan. Wipe out Satan? Perhaps they were going to get some of the latest detergents and spread it on a new floorcloth, or something, and try to rub out old Satan that way. Anyway all that garbage went where it should go – in the garbage.

There must be negative or there cannot be positive. There must be opposites or there is no motion. Everything that exists has motion. Night gives way to day, day gives way to night; summer gives way to winter, winter gives way to summer, and so on. There just has to be motion, there just have to be extremes. It's not bad to have extremes, it just means that two points are separated from each other as far as they can be. So, good old Satan, keep him going for a time because without Satan there could be no God, without God there could be no Satan because there wouldn't be any humans either. The worst 'Satan' is the awful driveller who tries to ram some religion down the throat of a person of another religion. I am a Buddhist, and I definitely resent all the stupid creeps who send me Bibles, New Testaments, Old Testaments, pretty pictures, purely imaginary of course (or should it be 'impurely'?) of Crucifixions, etc., etc., *ad lib*, *ad nauseam*. I am a Buddhist. All right, I am an extreme from Christianity, but Christians are extreme from me as a Buddhist. I do not try to get any converts to Buddhism, in fact a vast number of people write and ask me if they can become Buddhists, and my invariable answer is that they should remain affiliated with the religion to which they were born unless there is some great, great overriding condition or circumstance.

I do not like people who change their religion just because it is 'the done thing', or the newest thing, or because they want a thrill and have people point them out saying, 'Look, he's a Buddhist!'

But without the darkness there can be no sunshine. Yes, Mr. Announcer with the Cockney voice, you certainly said a great truth there. Don't let's persecute old Satan so much, he's got to live otherwise there is no standard of comparison, is there? If there was no talk of Satan, how would you judge good? If there was no bad there could be no good. Obviously not, because there would be no standard of comparison, because one must be able to compare X with Y, then we have good and bad just as in U.S.A. and Canada, it seems, there have to be 'good guys' and 'bad guys'. The good guys are always the red-blooded he-men, all American with Ivy League suits and the Pepsodent smile, whereas the bad guy is automatically the poor Indian who was swindled out of his country with a lot of specious promises. But think of the television programme, wouldn't it be dull if there were no good guys who could fight against the bad guys, or if there were no bad guys who could show how good the good guys really were? So, to all you people who write in and say don't I think Satan should be bumped off or rubbed out or excommunicated or sent to Russia, or something, let me say now – No, I think Satan is a good guy in that he provides a fall guy for good, he provides a standard against which we can measure good. So let's drink a toast to Satan, but just for luck let's have some sulphuric acid and brimstone in a glass and tip it upside down, it's safer that way.

The Old Man groaned as he unfolded the letter, 'I wrote to England for a Touch Stone,' he read, 'four weeks it was and I sent them the money, but I haven't had an answer. I think I am being swindled.'

The Old Man groaned aloud. Then he looked at the envelope and groaned again. First of all the Old Man is not in any way connected or interested in any business concern or venture. Sometimes a firm will branch out and claim that it is associated with Lobsang Rampa, etc., etc. There is only one case, and that is with a firm in England. They have permission to use the name of The Rampa Touch Stone Company. But, again, the Old Man wants to make it very, very clear that he is not connected with nor interested in any business enterprise. There is one firm with whom the Old Man is extraordinarily displeased because they advertise a mail order company using the name of the Old Man's first book, entirely without his permission, definitely with his disapproval.

So, there it is, that's business for you.

But the Old Man groaned as he looked at the envelope, and he groaned because neither on the envelope nor on the letter was there any address. In the U.S.A. and Canada people sometimes put their name and address on the envelope but rarely on the letter where it should be. In England and Europe the letter sheet itself bears the name and address of the sender, and so one can always reply to letters from England and Europe, yet this particular person groaning so bitterly and so libellously about being swindled had no address to which one could reply. What should one do then? The signature was just 'Mabel', nothing else, no surname, no address, and the postmark – well, that could not be read even with a magnifying glass. So you people who complain that you have had no reply who complain that you are being swindled, ask yourself – Did you really put your address on the letter or on the envelope?

A little time ago we had a letter and we couldn't read a single word of it. Probably it was in English, but we just couldn't read any part of it, so it had to go unanswered. The purpose of a letter is to make something known, and if the writing cannot be read the letter fails in its purpose, and if there is no address on it, well, it is just a waste of time.

The Old Man listening to his programme, the Overseas Programme of the B.B.C., pondered upon sounds. A few years back music was a very pleasant thing, a soothing thing or a rousing thing, but now – what has happened to the world? The stuff that is coming from England is like a horde of tomcats with their tails tied together. It isn't music, I don't know what it is. But sounds, well, different sounds are peculiar to different cultures. People have certain sounds which are alleged to do them good, such as the sound of 'OM' correctly pronounced. Yet there are other sounds which are not socially acceptable. The sounds of certain four letter words, for example, are not socially acceptable, and yet perhaps those same sounds are absolutely permissible in the language of another culture. There is a certain four letter sound which is naughty, naughty, very naughty indeed in English, and yet the sound in Russian is perfectly correct, perfectly decent, and used many many times a day.

Do not place too great a reliance on sounds. Many people get almost demented wondering if they are pronouncing 'OM' correctly. Of itself 'OM' is nothing, it doesn't mean a thing – of itself, not even if you pronounce it as it should be pronounced in Sanskrit. It is useless to pronounce a 'metaphysical word of power' correctly unless you also think correctly.

Consider this; think of your radio programme. You have certain sounds which, of themselves, cannot be transmitted. Those sounds can only be transmitted if first of all you have a carrier wave. A carrier wave is similar to the light you have

30

to show before you can transmit a cine picture or a television picture, or show your slides on a screen. The slides themselves, without light, are nothing. You have to have a light beam as a carrier, and in precisely the same way you have to have a carrier wave before you can transmit your radio programme.

Again, in exactly the same way the sound of 'OM', etc., or some other 'word of power' merely acts as a carrier wave to correct thoughts.

Do you want it made clearer? All right. Suppose we made a phonograph record which had nothing but 'OM' correctly pronounced, 'OM, OM, OM, OM, OM,' you could play that record for ever and a day provided it did not wear out first, and you just wouldn't do any good because the phonograph player, or gramophone, if you happen to be in England, is an unthinking machine. OM is useful only when one is thinking correctly as well as 'sounding' correctly. The best way to improve is to get one's thoughts right and let the sound take care of itself.

Sounds! What a powerful thing a sound can be. It can add impetus to one's thoughts. Music, good music, can stir one and lift one up spiritually. It can lead one to a greater belief in the honesty of one's fellows. Surely that is a most desirable attainment in itself. But music specially designed can make a rabble into a warlike army. Marching songs can help one march correctly and with less effort. But now – what's happened to the world? What's all this stuff worse than jazz, worse than rock 'n' roll? What's happened that young people are trying to drive themselves crazier with discordant cacophony which seems to be designed to bring out all the worst in them, drive them to drug addiction, drive them to perversions, and all the rest of it. That's what happens, you know.

People subjected to the wrong sound can have a longing for drugs. Drinking songs can make people desire to drink more, some of the old German biergarten songs were much the same as salted nuts provided, apparently, by some bars to increase the thirst and enable one to drink more to the greater glory of the publicans' income.

Now there are wars, revolutions, and hatreds and disturbances all over the world. Man fights against Man, and things will get much worse before they get much better. Sounds, bad sounds, cause it. Screaming, ranting agitators rousing the worst thoughts in the rabble just as Hitler, a most gifted but distorted orator, was able to rouse normally staid, sensible Germans to a frenzy, to an orgy of destruction and savagery. If only we could change the world by eliminating all the discordant music, all the discordant voices who preach hate, hate, hate. If only people would think love and kindness and consideration for others. There is no need for things to go on as they are. It needs just a few determined people of pure thought to produce those necessary sounds in music and in speech as would enable our poor sorely stricken world to regain some semblance of sanity instead of all the vandalism and juvenile delinquency which assails us daily. Then, too, there should be some censorship of the press for the press always, almost without exception, strives to make things appear more sensational, more bloodthirsty, more horrendous than really is the case.

Why not all of us have a period of meditation, thinking good thoughts, thinking and also saying good thoughts? It's so easy because the power of sound controls the thoughts of many people. Sound, provided it has a thought behind it.

The Old Man lay back in his bed, the poor fellow had no choice. Miss Cleopatra was lying on his chest with her head nestling in his beard, purring contentedly she gazed up with the bluest of blue eyes. Miss Cleopatra Rampa, the most intelligent of people, the most loving and unselfish of people, just a little animal to most people, although an exceptionally beautiful animal. To the Old Man this was a definite, intelligent Person, a Person who had come to this Earth to do a specific task and who was doing it nobly and with entire success. A Person with whom the Old Man had long telepathic conversations, and he learned much from her.

In the electric wheel chair Miss Tadalinka Rampa was curled up snoring away, every so often her whiskers would twitch and her eyes would roll beneath her closed eyelids. Taddy was a most affectionate Person, and Taddy loved comfort, comfort and food were Taddy's main preoccupations, and yet Taddy earned her food and her comfort. Taddy, the most telepathic of cats, did her share in keeping in touch with various parts of the world.

There came a light tap at the door and Friendly Neighbour came in and plonked a solid behind with a resounding 'thwack' upon a seat which seemed inadequate to contain such bulk. 'Love your cats, don't you Guv?' said Friendly Neighbour with a smile.

'Love them? Good gracious, yes! I regard them as my children, and as remarkably intelligent children at that. These cats do more for me than humans.'

By now Tadalinka was alert, sitting up ready to growl, ready to attack if necessary because both little cats can be very very fierce indeed in defence of what they regard as their responsibilities. At one apartment a man had tried to enter at night. Both cats had rushed to the door and nearly scared ten years of growth on to the poor fellow, because a Siamese cat in a fury is quite a frightening sight. They puff out, every hair of their fur stands straight out at right angles to the body, their tails fluff out, they stand on tiptoe and they look like something out of the inferno. They should not be called cats really because they are unlike cats. They roar, growl and fume, and nothing is too dangerous for a Siamese cat protecting a person or property. There are many legends about protecting by Siamese cats, many legends originating in the East about how this or that Siamese cat protected important people or sick people. But – enough. No one else tried to enter our apartment without our knowledge, the story of 'the fierce Rampa cats' went the round, and people are more frightened of wild Siamese cats than they are of mad dogs, it seems.

So it was, or, should it be, now it is, that now with the Old

Man so disabled the two little cats are ever alert to rush to his defence.

Oh yes, among our questions, here is a question from a lady who asks about animals. Where is it now? Ah, here! 'Can you tell us what happens to our pets when they leave this Earth? Are they utterly destroyed, or do they eventually reincarnate as humans? The Bible tells us that only humans go to Heaven. What have you to say about it?'

Madam, I have a lot to say about it. The Bible was written a long time after the events related happened, the Bible is not the original Writings either. It is a translation of a translation of a translation of another translation which had been re-translated to suit some king or some political power, or something else. Think of the King James Edition, or this Edition or that Edition. A lot of things written in the Bible are bunk. No doubt there was a lot of truth in the original Scriptures, but a lot of things in the Bible now are no more truth than the truth of the press, and anyone knows what a lot of bilge that is.

The Bible seems to teach humans that they are the Lords of Creation, that the whole world was made for Man. Well, Man has made an awful mess of the world, hasn't he? Where are there not wars, or rumours of wars, where is there no sadism, no terror, no persecution? You will have to move off this Earth if you want an answer to that. But we are dealing with animals and what happens to them.

In the first case there are many different species of creatures. Humans are animals, whether you like it or not humans are animals, horrid, uncouth, unfriendly animals, more savage than any of the Nature type animals.

Because humans have a thumb and fingers they have been able to develop along certain lines because they can use their hands to fabricate things, and that animals cannot do. Man lives in a very material world and only believes that which he can grasp between his fingers and his thumb. Animals, not having thumbs and not being able to grasp a thing in two hands, have had to evolve spiritually, and most animals

34

are spiritual, they do not kill unless for the absolute necessity of eating, and if a cat 'terrorizes and tortures' a mouse – well, that is an illusion of the human; the mouse is quite oblivious of it because it is hypnotized and feels no pain. Do you like that?

Under stress a person's sensations are anaesthetized, so in times of war, for example, a man can have an arm shot off and apart from a very dim numbness, he will not feel it until loss of blood makes him weak. Or a person piloting a plane, for instance, can be shot through the shoulder but he will go on piloting his plane and bring it down safely and only when the excitement has ended will he feel pain. In the case of our mouse by that time the mouse doesn't feel anything any more.

Horses do not reincarnate as daffodils. Marmosets do not reincarnate as maggots or vice versa. There are different groups of Nature people, each one in a separate isolated 'shell' which does not impinge upon the spiritual or astral existence of others. What that really means is that a monkey never reincarnates as a man, a man never reincarnates as a mouse although, admittedly, many men are mouse-like in their lack of intestinal fortitude which is a very polite way of explaining – well, you know what.

It is a definite statement of fact that no animal re-incarnates as a human. I know humans are animals as well, but I am using the accepted, the commonly accepted term. One refers to humans and one refers to animals because humans like to be buttered up a bit, and so one pretends that they are not animals but a special form of creature, one of God's chosen – humans. So – the human animal never, never reincarnates as a canine animal or feline animal, or equine animal. And, again, our old friend vice versa.

The human animal has one type of evolution which he must follow, the – which shall we say? – has a different, and not necessarily parallel, form of evolution to follow. So they are not inter-changeable entities.

Many Buddhist Scriptures refer to humans coming back

as spiders or tigers or something else, but of course that is not believed by the educated Buddhist, that started as a misunderstanding many centuries ago in much the same way as there is a misunderstanding about Father Christmas, or about little girls being made of sugar and spice and all things nice. You and I know that all little girls are not nice; some of them are *very* nice, some of them are proper stinkers, but, of course, you and I, we only know the nice ones, don't we?

When a human dies the human goes to the astral plane about which we shall say more later, and when an animal dies it, too, goes to an astral plane where it is met by its own kind, where there is perfect understanding, where there is perfect rapport between them. As in the case of humans, animals cannot be bothered by those with whom they are incompatible, and now study this carefully; when a person who loves an animal dies and goes to the astral world, that person can be in contact with the loved animal, they can be together if there is absolute love between them. Further, if humans were more telephatic, if they were more believing, if they would open their minds and receive, then loved animals who had passed over could keep in touch with the humans even before the humans passed over.

Let me tell you something; I have a number of little people who have passed over, and I am still very definitely, very much in contact with them. There is one little Siamese cat, Cindy, with thom I am in daily contact, and Cindy has helped me enormously. On Earth she had a very bad time indeed. Now she is helping, helping, always helping. She is doing absolutely as much as anyone on the Other Side can do for anyone on this Side.

Those who truly love their so-called 'pets' can be sure that when this life has ended for both, then they can come together again, but it's not the same.

When humans are on the Earth they are a disbelieving crew, cynical, hard, blasé and all the rest. When they get to the Other Side they get a shake or two which enables them to realize that they are not the Lords of Creation they thought they were, but just part of a Divine Plan. On the Other Side they realize that others have rights as well, when they get to the Other Side they find that they can talk with utmost clarity to animals who are also on the Other Side, and animals will answer them in any language they care to use. It is a limitation on humans that most of them while on Earth are not telepathic, most of them, while on Earth, are not aware of the character and ability and powers of so-called 'animals'. But when they pass over it all comes clear to them, and humans then are like a person born blind who suddenly can see.

Yes, animals go to Heaven, not the Christian Heaven, of course, but that is no loss. Animals have a real Heaven, no angels with goosefeathers for wings, it's a real Heaven, and they have a Manu, or God, who looks after them. Whatever Man can obtain or attain on the Other Side, so can an animal – peace, learning, advancement – anything and everything.

Upon the Earth man is in the position of being the dominant species, dominant because of the fearful weapons he has. Unarmed a man would be no match for a determined dog; armed with some artificial method such as a gun, a man can dominate a whole pack of dogs, and it is only through Man's viciousness that the telepathic power of communication with animals has been lost, that is the real story of the Tower of Babel, you know. Mankind was telepathic for general use, and mankind used speech only in local dialects for communicating with members of the family when they did not want the community as a whole to know what was being said. But then Man lured animals into traps by false telepathy, by false promises. As a result mankind lost the telepathic power as a punishment, and now only a few people on this Earth are telepathic, and for those of us who are it is like being a sighted person in the country of the blind.

Well, madam, to answer the question in your letter briefly – No, humans do not reincarnate as animals, animals do not

37

reincarnate as humans. Yes, animals go to Heaven, and if you truly love your pet then you can be together after you pass over IF your love is truly love and not just selfish, senseless desire to dominate or possess. And, finally on this subject, animals are not an inferior species. Humans can do a vast number of things that animals cannot, animals can do a vast number of things that humans cannot. They are different, and that's all there is to it – they are different, but not inferior.

Now, Miss Cleo, resting so comfortably, looked up with those limpid blue eyes and sent a telepathic message: 'To work, we have to work or we do not eat.' So saying she rose gracefully and most delicately walked off. The Old Man, with a sigh, turned to another letter and another question.

'Are there Mantras for sending dying animals to higher realms, and, if so, what are such Mantras?'

One doesn't need Mantras from humans to animals; just as humans have their own helpers waiting on the Other Side of life to help the dying human to be reborn back into the astral, so animals have their own helpers. And so there are no Mantras necessary to help dying animals enter the astral world. Anyhow animals know by instinct, or by pre-knowledge, far more about such things than do humans.

One should not wait until an animal is dying before one is ready to help. The best way to help an animal is while it is alive and well on this Earth because animals are beautiful creatures, and there are no bad or vicious animals unless they have been made bad and vicious by the ill-treatment, conscious or otherwise, of humans. I have known many cats, and I have never known a cat who was naturally vicious or bad tempered. If a cat has been tormented by humans, or by human children most likely, then of course it does adopt a protective fierceness, but soon with a little kindness all that goes, and one has a gentle, devoted animal again.

You know, a lot of people are scared stiff about Siamese cats, saying how fierce they are, how destructive, how everything bad. It isn't true, there isn't a word of truth in it, not a word. Miss Cleopatra and Miss Tadalinka never, never do anything to annoy us. If something irritates us, then we just say, 'Oh, don't do that, Clee!' and she doesn't do it again. Our cats do not tear up furniture or draperies because we have a pact with them; we provide a very easily made scratching post, actually we have two. They are sturdy posts, strongly mounted on a square base, both are covered with heavy carpet, not old scruffy carpet on which one has upset the garbage pail, but new carpet, actually off-cuts. Well, this carpeting has been securely fixed to the posts and on top of the posts there is room for a cat to sit.

Several times a day Cleopatra and Tadalinka go to their scratch posts, and they have such a long beautiful stretch that it makes one feel better just to watch. Sometimes they will walk up the post instead of jumping to the top, and that is very good for their muscles and very good for their claws. So, we provide the scratch posts and they provide the tranquillity because we do not have to fear for any furniture or any draperies.

Once I thought of writing a book about Cat Legends and the real story of cats. I'd love to, but increasing decrepitude makes it improbable that I ever shall. I would like to tell, for instance, how, on another world, in another system, far removed from the solar system, there was a high civilization of cats. In those days they could use their 'thumbs' as humans could, but, just as humans are doing now, they fell from grace and they had a choice of starting a Round all over again or going to another system to help a race not yet born.

Cats are kind creatures and understanding creatures, and so the whole race of cats and the Manu of cats decided to come to the planet we call Earth. They came to watch humans and report to other spheres on the behaviour of humans, something like having a television camera watching all the time, but they watch and report not to harm humans, but to help them. In the better regions people do not report things to cause harm but only so that defects may be over-come.

Cats came to be naturally independent so they would not be swayed by affection. They came as small creatures so that humans could treat them kindly or treat them harshly, according to the nature of the humans.

Cats are benign, a good influence on Earth. Cats are a direct extension of a Great Overself of this world, a source of information where much information is distorted by world conditions.

Be friendly with cats, treat them kindly, have faith in them knowing that no cat has ever willingly harmed a human, but very very many cats have died to help humans.

Well, Miss Tadalinka has just rushed in with a telepathic message, 'Hey, Guv, guess what? There's seventy-eight letters for you today!' Seventy-eight letters! It's about time I got down to answering some which are waiting.

CHAPTER THREE

The right Path is close at hand
yet mankind searches for it afar.

'WHAT is life like in Lhasa today? Are novices having their "third eye" opened? What has happened to all the people you describe in the first book?'

The Lhasa of 1970 under the terrorist rule of the Red Chinese is very, very different from the Lhasa of the era before the Chinese invasion. People are furtive, people look over their shoulders before venturing to speak to even the closest acquaintance. There are no beggars in the streets now; they have either been nailed up by their ears and are long since dead, or they have been sent to forced labour. Women are not the happy, carefree people they used to be. Now in Chinese dominated Tibet women are forcibly mated with Chinese men who have been deported from China and sent to Tibet to be the first colonists.

The Chinese are guilty of genocide, they are trying to kill the Tibetan nation. Chinese men were torn from their families in China and sent to Tibet to till the hard soil and to scrape a living somehow, sent to Tibet to mate with unwilling women and to be the fathers of a race of half-breeds, half Chinese and half Tibetan. As soon as a child is born it is taken away from the parents and placed in a communal home where it is taught as it grows up to hate all things Tibetan and to worship all things Chinese.

Tibetan men are being dealt with so that they are men no longer, so that they can no longer be fathers. Many men, and many women too, have escaped perhaps to India or perhaps to the higher mountain recesses where the Chinese

41

troops cannot climb. The Tibetan race will not die out, the Tibetan race will continue. It is a tragedy that the high ranking Tibetans now in India do not stir up interest in saving Tibet.

At one time I had the fond hope that some of these higher-ups would put aside their petty jealousies and petty hatreds and they would have co-operated with me. I have long had the great desire to speak as a representative of Tibet before the United Nations. I am not dumb, I am not illiterate, I know the side of the East and I know the side of the West, and it has long been my most fervent desire to serve Tibet by appealing to the Free Peoples of the world on behalf of the people now enslaved, now facing determined attempts to extinguish the whole race. But unfortunately I have been called many things, and those higher-ups, living in comfort in India, have not seen fit to do much about saving Tibet. However, that is another matter, and is 'one man's ambition', an ambition, though, which is entirely unselfish for I sought nothing for myself.

My books are true, every single one of them, they are absolutely true, but unfortunately the press saw fit to attack me, after all it's so much easier and so much more sensational for the press to try to pull down a person and try to make a blood-and-thunder tale out of something which doesn't exist than to admit the truth. It seems to me, looking back through the years, that those high ranking Tibetans in India, now living there in considerable comfort, are afraid to support me in the mistaken idea that if they did so they would lose the support of the press. Who cares about the press, anyhow? I don't!

People I have known in Tibet? The most highly placed of them have been killed, tortured to death. For example, Tibet's Prime Minister was dragged behind a speeding car through the streets of Lhasa, a rope was tied around one ankle, the other end of the rope was tied to the back of a car. The car was loaded with jeering Chinese, and off it started pulling an eminent man through the streets, turning and twisting on the rocky road, tearing off his nose, tearing off his ears, tearing off other things, until, raw-red and soaking with blood, he was just tossed aside on a garbage heap for dogs to devour.

Women whom I knew? Well, their daughters have been publicly raped in front of their families as well. Many eminent women have been forced into brothels for Chinese troops. The list could go on long about such happenings, but there is no point in it.

Certain cowardly men of high estate capitulated to the Chinese demands and became lackeys of the Chinese, obeying their every whim, aping them, fawning upon them, and remaining in positions of 'trust' until their masters tired of them and liquidated them.

Yet others escaped into the mountains to continue the fight against the Chinese. Many, of course, went to India. Well, that's their choice, but again the thought comes – why would not the Great Ones, safely in India, do something to help those who were not safe?

In the Great Temples and at the Potala itself all the gold sheets forming the roof have been torn off and carried away to China where, presumably, the gold has been melted down and made into money or something. Sacred Figures have been melted down for their gold and silver content, precious jewels have been removed and taken to China, and other things, books, manuscripts, paintings and carvings, have been tossed upon a great bonfire and the whole lot burnt up, and with it the history of a harmless, innocent country devoted only to the good of mankind.

Lamaseries are now brothels or barracks. Nunneries – well, the Chinese regard them as ready-made brothels. Ancient monuments have been torn down to afford easier passage for armoured columns.

Lhasa now is the capital city of terror, where people are tortured and killed without knowing the reason why. All that was beautiful has been destroyed. Unless alert men could save those things in time, and painfully carry them

43

off to mountain refuges where they would be stored for coming generations, all that was beautiful has been destroyed. Tibet will rise again, there is no final battle until the last battle, and only the last battle is decisive. Tibet will rise again. Perhaps there will be some strong man emerge who will be a great Ruler, perhaps he will re-vitalize those who now have merely sought safety and comfort in flight.

Tibet now is ringed with great roads, great barrack-like buildings housing workers who are trying to make some sort of order out of high barren land. It is not a happy task because the Chinese men, who have been forced against their own wishes to be immigrants or colonists, hate the land, hate the people, all they desire is to return to their own homes, to their own families. But the Tibetans are treated as sub-humans, the Chinese colonists are treated as prisoners and kept in Tibet against their will, and any who try to escape are tortured and publicly executed.

Meanwhile the nations of the world go about their own everyday business of having a few wars here and there – Korea, Viet Nam, Israel and the Arab countries, Africa, the Chinese/Russian border, and quite a few other places. But if there was a suitable Voice perhaps some of the more astute nations of the world would listen to a plea for help from an accredited representative of Tibet who could augment the spoken word by the written word, who could appear before the United Nations, who could appear on television, and who could write and write seeking aid for a stricken people before it is too late.

From the corridor came a roaring like a town bull on double overtime. A crash at the door and Outsize Neighbour came striding in. Face flaming like the setting sun he plonked down on a chair with a crash that seemed to shake the building. 'Know what?' he bellowed; 'those —'s in Halifax want to put up my rent!'

The Old Man, propped up in bed, tried to think of some good words to say about 'Halifax', but he had to admit that

44

everything was going up, milk, rent, postal charges, freight charges, the works!

Downstairs in the main lobby the Superintendent, Angus Robichaud, worked hard at cleaning the carpet. So much to do, far too much to do and far too much responsibility. Angus Robichaud is a good man, a loyal man, and one who successfully treads the narrow path between doing what his employers demand and doing as much as he can for his tenants. A rare man, of a type becoming increasingly hard to find.

In the Superintendent's Apartment his Wife, Mrs. Robichaud, was fighting to preserve patience and sanity between conflicting telephone calls. Mrs. Schnitzelheimer of 1027 was calling bad-temperedly: 'I vant ze 'eat you should turn off yes, already. My 'usband 'e say 'e got fried on 'is skin the 'eat she is too much, yes.' No sooner had she hung up with a bad-tempered bang than the 'phone rang again. 'Say, Ma'am, you just tell your husband to turn up that heat a lot pronto or I 'phone the Boss and make a complaint. What you think I pay for here, eh? To be refrigerated?'

Everything going up? The Old Man guessed that Mr. Robichaud's pay was not. What a pity, he thought, that some of these Apartment Building owners were so blind that they put a man in charge of a building that cost a few million to build – and probably pay him hardly enough to keep body and soul together. Yes, prices were going up to make money for those who already had plenty!

Pay? Pay? The price of everything is going up? Yes, that's a good question. I am asked why do occultists expect to be paid for giving advice, for information. It's wrong to charge for occult knowledge.

All right, Mrs. So-and-So, you go along to your lawyer or to your doctor or to your food store, go anywhere you like, and if you expect something you will have to pay for it. Your lawyer had to pay a lot of money for this training, he had many lean years as a student, and as a graduate lawyer. He invested money and time in knowledge, specialized knowledge, and he expects, and rightly expects, to have an adequate return on his investment.

Your doctor also had many years of hardship as a medical student. He had to study, he had to walk the wards, and then he had to pass a severe medical examination to see how much he knew and how little he knew. If he is any good as a doctor he is still studying, still keeping up with current developments, still reading about the results of research. He spent a lot of money on his studies, invested in the future, and like the lawyer, like a stockbroker, like anyone, he expects to get an adequate return on his investments.

Try going to a local store and getting free groceries. Tell the storekeeper it's criminal for him to have so much food upon his shelves while you have none on yours, tell him that it's criminal – him with so much food and you with none – for him to charge you. Do that, and you'll probably find yourself hustled off to the local mental home as being *non-compos mentis.*

The genuine occultist or metaphysician – and I am one – has spent a long time learning and suffering. As such, while we gladly do anything we can to help people, we still have the right to live, the right to eat, the right to wear clothes, as such we make a charge. Ask your doctor, your grocer, or your lawyer if that is not correct.

There is another question on the same letter; perhaps we should deal with that at the same time; it is pertinent to the remarks above.

The question is – 'I have been to Vancouver and I live in British Columbia. There is a man there who charges large sums of money for answering questions. He says he is a student of yours, and he works very closely with you and you advise him whenever he is in difficulties. This man has taken a lot of money from me, and he has given me information which is completely and utterly false. What have you got to say about that?'

In the first case, I am not working with anyone. I have no

46

students whatever. It is utterly false to say that I am working closely with any fortune-teller; I don't believe in fortune-tellers. Too often if one 'fortune tells' one induces a person to do what he or she would not normally do, but we will deal with that in a moment.

If you have reason to believe that person is posing as a student of mine and that person is obtaining money from you by falsely pretending to be a student of mine, then all you have to do is to go to the local Police Station and see someone in the local Fraud Squad. Explain things to him, and if you like you can show him this book, show him this page, where I state most definitely that I have no students whatever and that I do not work at all with fortune-tellers or anyone of that ilk.

Tell him also that I have no disciples, I do not want disciples, actually they are a darn nuisance! But, of course, that's between you and me. Disciples bumble around, 'Yes Master this, yes Master that,' they get under foot, they creep out from the woodwork like termites. So many, many years ago I decided that I would never have students and I would never have disciples, and all this makes your fortune-teller in Vancouver, British Columbia, sound a bit silly, doesn't it? No madam, don't blame me for false information. I give none, I don't even sell any. I write my books, and here again you have my positive, my definite statement, that all my books are true. I wouldn't swear it on a stack of Bibles because I am not a Christian and that would not mean any more to me than swearing on a bundle of old newspapers, but, I repeat, all my books are true.

It's unwise, you know, to bother with fortune tellers. After all, each and every one of us comes to this Earth as students to a school. Now supposing you went to College and during a vacation or half day off you puttered over to some old biddy who probably wears great big earrings and a scarf over her head, and you said in effect, 'Hi, Biddy, what am I going to do next term? I won't tell you anything, you tell me all.' Well, the old biddy couldn't tell you much, could she? She wouldn't know what course you were taking, she wouldn't know what your secret ambitions were, what your weaknesses were. No! And the average fortune-teller is much like that.

Now, read this carefully, get it engraved on your memory; no human can consult the Akashic Record of another human without 'Divine Permission'. And you can take it that Divine Permission is rarer than hair on an egg, so if people say they are just going to buzz off for a moment, have a look at the Akashic Record and come back with a blueprint of your past life and your future life, just tell them what you think and if you are wise just call in the Fraud Squad if any money is involved.

Every one of us is here to do something, and if we listen to fortune-tellers who do not really know what they are telling, then we might be side-tracked and instead of making a success of our life we may be heartily disillusioned, discouraged, or disenchanted. The best thing is to meditate properly, and if you do that you can know an awful lot about yourself – and usually it is quite awful. You see things where you have gone wrong through listening to others. Of course, you can *listen* to others, but you have to make a choice yourself and go your own way with full responsibility for yourself.

One of the most foolish statements ever made is to the effect that no man is an island unto himself. Silly, isn't it? Of course everyone has to be 'an island unto himself'.

If you join cults and groups, then you are not being an individual you are being just somebody living in a community. If you become a member of a cult or group you are not accepting your responsibility as an individual human. No doubt this will cause a considerable uproar among all those people who advertise metaphysical correspondence courses where you pay high sums for life and get little back, but the whole truth is this: no matter what your mother told you to do, no matter what your group leader told you to do, or the high mystical holder of the symbolic key of the correspondence college, when you pass over from this life you, and *you* alone have to answer to your Overself for what you did or for what you did not do. It is utterly futile for you to think that you can say, 'Oh, you can't blame me for that, I only did what my mother told me to do. If she were here she would tell you so herself.' But that is idiotic. You have to take the responsibility, and you alone. So, if you have to take the responsibility, and you most certainly have, then why allow yourself to be persuaded to do something by a gang of people who are out to get your money or out to get a bit of power through heading a group? That type of person is not going to stand by you when your Overself is judging your life. Again let me repeat, you, and *you* alone, have to answer to your Overself, so you, and you alone should live your life and make your decisions, and accept or reject responsibilities just as you and you alone think fit.

It is useless to listen to Mr. Dogwalloper, the President of the Hog's Tooth Metaphysical Society who will tell you this and tell you that and tell you something else, and who will tell you that if you do as his cult suggests you will get a reserved seat in Heaven with free harp playing lessons thrown in. You won't know. If Mr. Dogwalloper knew enough he wouldn't talk such a lot of bilge, he would be so busy trying to clear up his own life and preparing for his own judgment that he wouldn't meddle with your responsibilities.

In the same way it is stupid to be swayed or influenced by those old women of both sexes who prate and yowl that you should join their religious group, telling you how damned you will be if you don't, telling you how wonderful you will be if you do join them. Well, again, remember that all these people will not answer for you later.

Too many people bleat about 'God's blessing be upon you'. They come pretending that they have direct authority from God to bless one and to give one absolution for things already done. Well, God must be awfully busy! These people are just the same as you, and you, and you – no better and perhaps no worse. They might be deluded, they might think that because they wear their collar the wrong way round, or because they read a book, that they automatically have become a saint.

Having a knowledge of metaphysics does not necessarily make one spiritual, you know. According to legends old Satan himself knows quite a trick or two in the metaphysics line, but you are not going to call him spiritual, are you, not in the right way, that is. To come down to brass tacks, anyone can learn metaphysical things, it doesn't matter how bad the person, he or she can learn such things, he doesn't have to be of a certain degree of spirituality first. But a great and merciful Providence nearly always, not always but nearly always, arranges matters so that if we get a double-dyed villain studying metaphysics he changes first to a once-dyed villain and some of the dye washes out, he might even be a decent fellow beneath. But don't believe all the advertisements about the 'Saintly So-and-So who is now a Swami'. A Swami is a Mr., do you know that? It is no mystical title, that little word Swami really carries weight with a lot of people, but don't you be fooled by it.

Now, I see there is another question here which really we have just answered. The question is, 'Tell me why people shouldn't do metaphysical things in groups but should do it alone.'

I have already answered that, but perhaps I can add to it. A short time ago I was sent some 'literature' from a group who wanted me to join them. They boasted about their vast classes who were all meditating together. Did you ever read anything more stupid than that – 'who were all meditating together'? Well, if they had a scrap of metaphysical knowledge they would know what you can't meditate together. Do you know why?

Every human radiates energy, radiates waves, waves of thought, waves of prana, and everyone is to some extent telepathic, so if you get a whole group of people all meditating about their own affairs – well, they certainly do gum up the works and it is impossible to do any worthwhile meditation for oneself when in a group.

You get the same sort of thing in big crowds. Take a football crowd, for instance; here you get a few thousand normal people, some of them fairly well balanced, some of them as crazy as coots, and they all congregate together. They are thinking about the game, and then something happens, someone thinks a certain thing and says a certain thing, and here in this crowd you get a sudden group personality, you get mass hysteria. People get trampled underfoot, immense damage is done to the football ground buildings, seats collapse, people come storming out through the gates yelling and shouting, and roughing up any one in their path, and later, when the crowd breaks up, the responsible ones feel quite dreadful and shamefacedly they wonder whatever happened to them.

The same thing happens in group meditation. Everybody thinking on a certain thing can cause the law of Reversed Effort to take place. I said, 'thinking about the same thing'. The mere fact of meditation, of meditating is enough because if one is meditating then it is a definite act, and every person meditating adds his or her own grain to the newly formed thought form or group personality, and unless there are some highly trained people – there rarely are – who can control things, you get all sorts of nervous illnesses resulting from the meeting. So, again I say, if you want this to be your last life on this Round do not join groups or cults, live your own life, accept your own responsibilities, make your own decisions. Oh yes, by all means, consider the advice of others, consider advice, weigh up the different advice you get, and then decide for yourself. Then when you have left this Earth and you are in the Hall of Memories with your knees knocking together with fright, and you get the judgment of your Overself upon your sins of omission and commission, you might get a few words of praise for yourself, and you might come out thinking, 'Yes, yes, I'm glad I followed Lobsang Rampa's advice. He was right after all.'

With the closing of the day 'the Family' were gathered about the Old Man's bed. Miss Cleopatra was looking out at the ships in the harbour, Miss Tadalinka was sitting on the Old Man's lap. Ma put down the first pages of the typescript which she had been reading and almost simultaneously Buttercup put down the copy which she had been reading.

'Well?' queried the Old Man, 'What do you think of it?'

Ma rubbed her ear and said, 'It's all right, it made me laugh so that should be test enough.'

'And how about you, Buttercup, what do you think about it?' the Old Man said.

Buttercup – well, she looked down at the typescript again and then looked up at the Old Man as she said, 'You repeat yourself, you know. That bit about Metaphysicians getting paid, well, you said something like that in "Beyond the Tenth".'

'But sure I repeated myself,' said the Old Man in some exasperation. 'How do I know if the person who is reading this book has read "Beyond the Tenth"? And these things, to my mind, are so important that surely a repetition is justified. After all, if you go to school the teacher doesn't say a thing just once and expect you to have it for ever and three days, does he? He repeats it.'

Ma broke in – almost as if to prevent a fight! – 'You say about no disciples, about not being interested in anything, how about John?'

The Old Man remembered his blood pressure, remembered his various complaints and sat gamely on his safety valve – if bodies have safety valves – But anyway, he suppressed, as so often of late he had had to suppress, the various comments which rose almost unbidden.

'All right, we'll make an exception about John. All right, we'll clear up one or two things which you say are not adequately covered so far.' So – here goes.

Every so often one comes across a man or a woman who has a deep urge to obey spiritual impulses and to improve

52

the nature and show that Kharma can be overcome. Such a person is John Henderson. We are very fond of John Henderson – er, let me qualify that; his hobby is acting and he is a very good actor except when he tries to act the role of an Irish priest. His Irish accent is more like the Bronx in New York, that, though, is a digression. John Henderson is a good man who is trying and succeeding. I have suggested to him most strongly that later, when he is a bit older, he starts a Spiritual Retreat so that he can help those who need help. He won't be telling fortunes, he won't be trying to delude anyone. Instead, as a truly spiritual person he will be trying to help. So perhaps in three or four years you will be reading about John Henderson, in the best way of course, that's understood.

Buttercup said, 'But *how* does metaphysics help people to be more spiritual? You say that anyone can study metaphysics and usually even the bad ones turn good when they study metaphysics. How?'

Well, before the Communist take-over in Tibet there were various inscriptions carved on the lintels of lamasery entrances, such as 'A thousand monks, a thousand religions', or 'The saffron robe does not a monk make'. Unfortunately there are many arrant fakers and phoneys in occultism, so much is hard to disprove and so much appeals to what people want to know. Some of the bums who study metaphysics, or pretend to study metaphysics, gather a little knowledge and then act as if they were Gods who know everything, plus. Actually most of these people really are just that – ignorant bums and nothing more. They are not truly studying with the intention of progressing, they are not truly studying with the desire to help others. They are trying to get a fast-talking smattering of occultism so they can make a fast buck. They are just pursuing a cult or even trying to start a fresh cult. They set out with a gang of so-called 'disciples' and they perpetrate all sorts of spiritual crimes, they lead people astray and they divert people from what should be their real task.

At the present time, within the past very few years, a great horde of people have come on the scene, people whom one could justifiably call 'the great unwashed'. Most of them are not merely unwashed, they stink with it physically and spiritually. They seem to take a pride in wearing tattered rags of clothing, and they take an ever greater pride in being uncouth and coarse, well, uncouth is being coarse, isn't it? But anyway, they are uncouth and they are also coarse with it. Let me tell them, as I so often tell them in letters, that there is no virtue in being dirty, in fact with many of them I would like to get busy with a pig scraper and remove the first few layers of dirt to see what really was beneath.

Now for that question from Buttercup as to why people should study metaphysics; in studying metaphysics they are just getting back what should be a birth right. Metaphysics has a scruffy name, but that is because scruffy people have abused the name. Actually, in years gone by everyone had metaphysical ability, that is, everyone was clairvoyant and telepathic, but through abusing those powers they lost the ability, the ability atrophied. You get the same sort of thing with a person who has to stay in bed a long time. If a person is confined to bed and not permitted to exercise the leg, then the person loses the power of walking, forgets how to do it, and when the illness which caused the poor wretch to stay in bed has been cured he or she has to be taught to walk all over again.

A person who has been born blind and suddenly through some advance in science has been given sight, has to be trained in the art of seeing because when you see for the first time you cannot comprehend what it is that you are seeing. One has to be taught to see things in 3D, one has to be taught to be able to judge distances. On this I have much personal experience because I have been blind, and recovering sight suddenly is quite a shock.

So people study metaphysics so that they may regain powers which their ancestors had and lost. And how does metaphysics help even bad people become less bad

54

and more spiritual? Easy! When one studies metaphysics it actually raises a person's vibrations, and the higher a person's vibrations are the more spiritual he becomes. So if a real thug suddenly has a change of heart and starts to study metaphysics, the mere act of studying occult knowledge makes him a better man, while reducing his value as a thug.

CHAPTER FOUR

Success is the culmination of hard
work and thorough preparation.

'BUT why do crowds get out of control?' Buttercup would not let the question drop. 'You say that football crowds get out of control, well, we know that is so, but *why* do, *how* do they, what mechanism is employed?'

The Old Man gave a sigh because he wanted to discuss something quite different, but a question is a question, and there may be many people who are interested in *why, how,* etc.

Every person has a magnetic field around him – oh yes, naturally we include 'her' in that, and sad to relate all too frequently the magnetic field around the female of the species is stronger than that of the male. Possibly that is why the female of the species is supposed to be dangerous! Everyone, then, has a magnetic field around the body. This magnetic field is not the aura, it is the etheric, and if you find it difficult to visualize think that instead of a collection of people you have a collection of bar magnets. Naturally enough they will be standing on end the same as people do, so let us say the North points up and the South points down. Well, immediately you have a lot of magnets with their fields inter-acting, some are stronger, some are weaker, some are perhaps a bit warped, and together they build up quite a formidable force and they have a strong effect upon nearby structures.

In a very similar way humans, with their built-in magnets, interact upon each other. Some of the magnetic fields are disturbing fields rather opposed to others, and they will create a ripple of discontent which can grow and affect people who are normally quite sensible and stable. In a football crowd everyone is thinking more or less about the same thing, that is, about the game. Yes, we know that perhaps half the crowd want one side to win, and the other half want the other side to win, but we can disregard that because they are both thinking of substantially the same thing – 'a win'. So all the time the game is in progress the magnetic field is being increased, and increased, and increased by the positive thoughts of 'a win'. When some player does something wrong one side is overjoyed and gets a surge of power, while the other side is despondent and has a reverse of power which, again, causes a discordant note in what one might term the basic frequency of humans.

Under certain conditions mass hysteria is generated. People who are normally quite decent and well behaved lose control of themselves, and do things of which they are heartily ashamed after.

You know that everyone has a built-in censor, that 'little inner voice which keeps us on the straight and narrow path', and when mass hysteria occurs the Kundalini of people is affected and the reverse current (note carefully that it is a reverse current) surges along the spinal column, overpowering the good impulses of the Kundalini and overpowering and temporarily paralysing the human built-in censor.

With the censor overpowered there is no limit to the destruction, to the vandalism, and to the outright savagery of which a human is capable. Every fresh act seems to lend power. People become oblivious to hurts they receive themselves, they get bruises, cuts and assorted gashes in the melee, and they do not notice them.

The weaker people fall to the ground and are trampled on. Panic sets in and the whole mass of people will charge the exits or barricades, and by sheer weight of numbers will crash through leaving many injured behind them.

When the crowd disperses the magnetic build-up fails and

dissipates, and so people 'come to their senses'. Those who can get away to their own homes have time to feel heartily ashamed of themselves at home, whereas those who are carted off in a Black Maria or Paddy-Wagon, cool off in what the Police inelegantly term 'the cooler'. The cooler, of course, is a cell where hot tempers soon subside.

Oh yes, of course, on a lesser degree such things can occur with groups and cult meetings. You can get much the same sort of thing when a whole horde of people get together and imagine they are meditating, but they are not, they are building up quite a reversed current which does more harm than good.

Ladies and Gentlemen, those of good intention, those who try to do good for others, your attention please for something which is of vital importance to sufferers.

Do you ever try to do so-called 'absent healing'? Do you ever dash off a bunch of prayers for those who are afflicted? Do you think you are doing a lot of good helping to cure and all that? As a victim of such very well intentioned efforts I want to utter a shriek of protest on behalf of the sufferers.

Supposing one has three, or four, or five, or six people all wanting to do absent healing on to one poor sufferer. These three, four, five or six people may have absolutely the purest intentions but they do not know the exact nature of the illness afflicting the sufferer, they try to cast a blanket cure and, believe me, I have definitely been injured by such so-called blanket coverage.

It is very, very dangerous to hypnotize a person into believing that he has no illness when, in fact, he is almost dying from some complaint. It is equally dangerous to do this absent healing stuff unless you are a qualified doctor and know the nature of the disease and what side effects there can be from that disease. Again we have our old friend, or more likely, old enemy, the Law of Reversed Effort, with which to contend.

Under certain conditions if one too ardently desires a thing and one concentrates untrained thoughts on a certain thing, then instead of getting a positive thing, a positive result, one gets a negative result. When you get five or six people all doing the same thing the suffering of the victim – well, I've had some!

My strong recommendation based on the most unfortunate personal experience is that none of you try absent healing without knowing the precise nature of the complaint, without knowing what side effects might be expected, without knowing the severity of the complaint.

Have you ever been in a really populated area and tried to get a radio programme, and there seemed to be stations coming in from everywhere, each interfering with the others so the result was nothing but jangled cacophony with nothing clear in the whole bunch? That's what you get with absent healing. I do a lot of short wave listening, it's about my only entertainment now, and sometimes a station will be jammed by Russia or China, and the whining and wailing and weirdy-woos make one have to switch off in a hurry. Unfortunately it's not so easy to switch off when a group of people are trying ill-advisedly and in conflict with each other to do absent healing. Mind you, the people concerned can have the highest motives, but unless they are trained as priests or as medical practitioners it's a thing which cannot be recommended.

The other day a taxi driver asked Buttercup a question. He said, 'Don't you agree that young people today are far more alert and far more intelligent than were their fathers?' Buttercup had her own comments about that, and probably they were the same as the comments I make:

Do I think that young people of today are more aware than were their parents at a similar age?

No, by golly, I don't, I think they are a lot dimmer. I think some of them nowadays are just a gang of exhibitionists going about with their long hair and their scruffy tattered rags of clothing, and the stench which comes from them is enough to lift one's hat off. Not only that, but so many of them appear to be downright stupid.

A few years ago, when parents, or – no, let's go farther back – when grandparents were teenagers they had to work, they had to study, they couldn't go watching television all the time or blaring hi-fi. They had to do things, they had to make their own entertainments. It taught them to think. Nowadays young people do not seem able to make themselves understood in what should be their own language, they are illiterate, downright crummy in fact. There are some children nearby of school age and their command of English is not a command at all, its a complete disorder. They seem to be as illiterate as Hottentots who don't even know what school is.

Personally I think children and teenagers are going like this because both parents go out to work and ignore the absolutely essential requirement that the rising generation shall be taught by the generation whom they are replacing.

I think, too, that television and the cinema are largely to blame for the illiteracy and the general mental sluggishness of the average teenager.

The films, the television shows, well, they show an absolutely artificial world, an absolutely artificial set of conditions. They show wonderful houses, wonderful estates and fantastically expensive furnishings. and the film stars seem to have fleets of Cadillacs and hordes of boy friends or girl friends. Immorality is not merely condoned, it is actually encouraged. Actress Dinah Dogsbody, for instance, boasts of how many men she has run through and left weak-kneed and shaking, while actor Hector Hogwash boasts of having perhaps fourteen wives, presumably divorcing them one after the other, but anyway, what is the difference between prostitution and these actors and actresses who change partners almost at the drop of a – well, drop of a hat; I was going to say something different, but perhaps there are ladies reading this.

My answer, then, is that I think the general standard of education is falling rapidly. I think the education in Europe is far, far higher than it is in the U.S.A. and Canada, but then in Europe there is still some semblance of parental discipline.

Nowadays mere children can do a menial sort of job, work short hours and get enough money to run wild, to buy all sorts of expensive radios, to buy a car, and almost anything they set their mind to. If they do not have the cash then they soon get a credit account and they are hooked for life just as surely as if they were on drugs.

What is the point of giving people education when the major part of that education seems to be teaching them that they should have things which they have no possible chance of obtaining? I think there should be a return to religious discipline, not necessarily Christian, not necessarily Buddhist, not necessarily Jewish, but a return to some religion because until the world has some spiritual discipline, then the world will continue to turn out worse and worse specimens of humanity.

Quite a number of young people write to me and tell me I am an old fuddy-duddy because I do not approve of drugs. Now these young people, sixteen, seventeen or eighteen years of age, they think they know all, they think the whole fount of knowledge is open to them instead of realizing that they have hardly started to live, instead of realizing that they are hardly out of the egg.

I am definitely, utterly, and irrevocably opposed to drugs of any kind unless they are administered according to strict medical supervision.

If a person goes and chucks a dollop of acid in the face of another person, then the results are apparent, the flesh peels away, the eyes burn out, acid scores deep grooves in the chin and runs down to the chest, and the result is generally horrible. But that is a kindly act compared to what happens when people become drug addicts.

Drugs wrongly used, and all drugs used without medical supervision are wrongly used, can sear the astral body just as acid can sear the physical body.

61

A drug addict who dies and passes over to the astral world has a truly horrible time. He has to go to what is in effect an astral mental hospital because his astral body is warped and distorted, and it may take a long, long time before the most skilled attention that he can receive can restore that astral body to anything like a workable condition.

People rave about this entirely evil drug L.S.D. Think of the number of suicides there have been, the ones that are reported, and think of the ones that have not been reported, think of the harm that has been caused in terms of insanity and violence. L.S.D., marijuana, heroin, all those things, they are all devilishly evil. Unfortunately young people do not seem able to accept the advice of older people, people who have the experience.

It is true that, for example, L.S.D. will get the astral body separated from the physical body, but all too often, unfortunately, the astral body goes down to one of the lower hells, one of the weirdy astral planes, and when it comes back the subconscious itself is seared with the horrors it has undergone. So, young people who should be reading this, stay away from drugs, never mind if you do think drug X or drug Y is harmless, if they are taken without medical supervision, *you* might have some idiosyncrasy which will make you particularly susceptible to those drugs and very quickly you will be hooked beyond hope of recovery.

Remember, all these drugs are harmful, and although by some remote chance it might now show on your physical for the time being, yet it will show very definitely upon your astral and on your aura.

By the way, if people do take drugs and they damage their astral bodies, then they come under the same category as do suicides, and if a person commits suicide then he or she has to come back to this Earth to finish his or her sentence, which is one way of looking at it, or to complete his or her lessons, which is another way of looking at it. Whichever way you look at it there are no drop-outs from the Heavenly Fields, no drop-outs from this Earth either. If you gum up the works this time and do not learn the things which you came here to learn, then you come back and back and back again until you do learn your lessons. So this drug business is a very serious thing indeed and no action taken by the government can be in any way too severe to deal with the drug problem. The best way to deal with it is for each and every one of us to decide that *we* will not take drugs. In that way we shall not be spiritual suicides, and we shall not have to come back to this Earth into steadily worsening conditions.

In the last paragraph I referred to spiritual suicides – repeating the remarks in others of my books – about suicides. I receive an amazing number of letters from people who tell me that they are going to commit suicide. Perhaps they have been crossed in love, perhaps they weren't crossed in love and lived to regret it, but whatever it is I have been appalled at the number of people who write to me saying they are going to commit suicide. Let me state once again, as I have stated constantly, suicide is never, never justified. If one commits suicide one just gets slapped back to this Earth to 'enter class' once again. So, do not think that you can escape your responsibilities by cutting your throat or slashing your wrists, or anything like that; you can't.

Some years ago a boy who was somewhat unstable apparently committed suicide and left a note to say he was going to come back in a few years' time. Well, unfortunately, a copy of one of my books (*You – Forever*) was found near him, and the press really had a Roman holiday, they went delirious with joy, they raked up everything they could think of and then they called in other people to see if they could think of anything else. And, you know, the most amazing thing of all is that it was reported in the press that I encouraged suicide. Actually, I have never encouraged suicide. I often think I would like to murder press people, but that fate would be far too good for them. Let them go on making their mistakes and let them pay for it after. I personally believe that the majority of press people are subhuman. I personally believe that the press is the most evil force on this Earth today because the press distorts things and tries to whip up excitement or frenzy, tries to drive people to war. If Government leaders could sit down together and discuss matters without the press blaring out a collection of lies and ruining friendly relations, then we should have more peace. Yes, emphatically, based on my own experiences, I am firmly of the belief that the press is the most evil force on this world today.

I mention all this because even the press reported that the boy thought he would come back and start again. Well, that was right, the boy would have to come back again. But let me again repeat, I never, never encourage suicide. As I have stated unchangingly for the whole of my life, suicide is *never* justified, and while some Buddhists apparently do it in the belief that it is going to help the Buddhist cause or the cause of peace, I still maintain that suicide is never justified. So – my strong recommendation is do not even contemplate suicide, it doesn't help, you will have to come back under worse conditions. And if you stick it out here nearly always it's not so bad as one fears. The worst things of all never happen, you know, we only think they might.

Suicides, dead bodies, etc., etc. Now here is a question which came only yesterday. A lady asks, 'The cloud which stays over a body for three days – is it the soul or the astral body? Doesn't the soul leave soon for the Other Side?'

Well, yes, of course. The soul leaves the body with the cutting of the Silver Cord just the same as a child is entirely detached from its mother's body as the umbilical cord is detached. Until that umbilical cord is severed then the child is in co-existence with its mother. In the same way, until the Silver Cord is disconnected the astral body is co-existent with the physical body.

The cloud which hangs over a dead body for three days or so is just the accrued energy dissipating. Look at it in another way; suppose you have a cup of tea, the tea is poured out and before you can drink it you are called away.

The tea stays hot, but becomes cooler, and cooler, and cooler; so, in the same way, until the body has lost all the energy built up during the lifetime, a cloud hovers over the body gradually dispersing over three days. Another illustration; suppose you have a coin in your hot little hand and you suddenly put down that coin, the energy imparted in the form of heat from your hot little hand doesn't suddenly disperse, it takes a certain amount of time for the heat put in the coin by your hand to go, and for the coin to return to the ordinary temperature surrounding it. In the same way an astral body can be quite detached from the physical body, but by the principle of magnetic attraction it can still sense the charge around the physical body, and so until all that charge has gone it is said that the physical body and the astral body are connected.

One of the horrors of dying in this part of the world is the barbaric practice over here in North America of embalming people. It seems to me to be much the same as stuffing chickens, or something, so in my own case I am going to be cremated as that is far better than to be handled and messed around by the embalmer and his mate. And, as a certain lady cat said, 'The Old Man is trying to complete *Feeding the Flame* before he feeds the flame.' May I for my part say that I hope they will not put on the crematorium door (when I am inside) 'Frying tonight.'

A lady – I am sure she is a lady because she writes in such an elegant manner – takes me to task somewhat, 'Why do you occultists always say this is so, and that is so, but offer no proof? People must have proof. Why do you not give proof? Why should we believe anything? God has never said a word to me, and the astronauts have not seen any sign of heaven in space.'

Proof! That's one of the biggest things, but tell me this; if one is a sighted person in the country of the blind, how does one give proof that there is sight? Moreover, how do you give proof when so many people will not believe a thing when it's stuck slap in front of their nose?

There have been many very eminent scientists (I can only think of Sir Oliver Lodge for the moment), quite a number of famous names have been interested in proof, in science cooperating with the occult world. For example, Sir Oliver Lodge, a most spiritual man, addressed a very important Association in 1913 in England. Sir Oliver said, 'Either we are immortal beings or we are not. We may not know our destiny, but we must have a destiny of some sort. Science may not be able to reveal human destiny, but it certainly should not obscure it.' He went on to say that in his opinion the present-day methods of science would not work in secur-- ing proof. He said also that it was his belief that if reputable scientists were allowed to work free without all the scoffers and doubters, then they could reduce occult occurrences to physical laws, and that is obviously very much so. People who demand proof demand proof in the terms of bricks standing upon bricks, they want proof while all the time they are trying to prevent that proof. People who go into occult studies just trying to get a material proof are like people who go into a darkroom and turn on the lights to see if there is any image on the yet undeveloped film. Their actions definitely inhibit any manifestation of proof.

In the occult world we are dealing with intangible matters, we are dealing with matters of an extremely high vibration, and the way people go along nowadays is something like using a pneumatic road drill to excavate in order that fillings may be put in one's teeth. Before proof can be given in a materialistic sense scientists have to be trained in what can be and what cannot be, it's useless for them to charge like a bull at a gate, they are not breaking bricks, they are trying to find out something which is as basic as humanity itself. If people will be honest with themselves, if they will stay away from the television screens and the cinemas and all that stuff, and if they will meditate properly, then they will have an inner awareness that such a thing *is*, they will become aware of their own spiritual natures,

66

always assuming that their spiritual nature is not so debased as to preclude any other manifestation.

For years in addition to wanting to photograph the aura which I see around every person I have wanted to develop, as I have already stated, a telephone which would enable the ordinary people, non-clairvoyant, non-clairaudient people to telephone the Other Side. Think what fun it would be looking up a Heavenly telephone directory and having to ask for information – Did he go up or down? I suppose the nether regions would have an exchange called Brimstone, or something similar. Anyway, in years to come when scientists are less materialistic, then it will be that there will be such a telephone. Actually there has been, but that is another story.

Perhaps I should head the next bit 'Stop press news' because there has been a telephone call from John Henderson, some three thousand miles away. He has now had some proof of people on the Other Side of this life. A message came to him and he had the sensation that he was having his head kicked which is what I once told him I would like to do to him! But anyway, he just phoned to say that at last he has GOT THE MESSAGE. That message was directed from the Other Side and not at all impelled by me. Some day perhaps John Henderson may write a book, he should, and if he tells about this occurrence many people will probably say, 'Well, I never! I wouldn't like such things to happen to me!'

'Hi, Guv,' said Miss Taddy, jerking to a full awake after being soundly and noisily asleep for some time. 'I've got a question which any human would like answered.'

'All right, Tadikins, what is it?'

So Miss Tadikins sat down and folded her arms and said, 'Well, it's like this; we cats know what arrangements are made on the Other Side, but why don't you tell humans how they plan their life on Earth?'

Personally I thought I had dealt with that *ad nauseam*

and I don't want Buttercup to come jumping at me telling me that I am repeating myself, and after writing so much about suicide it might be something akin to suicide if I start up again writing about life after death, so perhaps I can get over it by calling this answer 'Life Before Birth'.

On the Other Side of this life an entity has decided that he or she must go to school again to take a special course. Perhaps certain lessons were learned previously and the return Home has enabled those lessons to be digested and weaknesses to be perceived. So then the entity who is he or she, sits down and thinks things over.

On Earth many students discuss their future with a counsellor, they discuss what courses are required in order that they shall obtain a certain qualification. For example, a nurse in England wants to become a surgeon; obviously she has some knowledge of anatomy, so what does she need in order to enter Medical School? She discusses what she has to do, and then goes to it. In the same way our he or she on the Other Side of life on Earth decides with considerable help what lessons have to be learned, what tasks have to be surmounted, and what difficulties have to be endured. Then the whole thing is planned very carefully.

Do you play chess? Well, if you do you will know all about those chess problems which appear in certain magazines. The chess board is all set up with pawns and knights and rooks, and all that, in certain predetermined positions. You, poor soul, have to think and think until your brain nearly cracks and work out a way in which to win that game. It's something like that in planning the life to come. All the obstacles are set up, all the conditions are laid down; what do you have to learn, do you have to learn poverty and how to overcome it? It's no good going to a rich family, then, is it? Do you have to learn how to be generous to others, how to handle money? Then it's no good going to a poor family, is it? You have to decide what you want to learn, you have to decide what sort of family will best meet your requirements. Are you coming to a tradesman's family or to a professional family? Or are you coming as one of a noble family? It all depends, you know. It's like actors on a stage, an actor may be a king in one play and a beggar in another, and it's just the same with life, it depends on what you have to learn. You come to the station, to the conditions, to the difficulties, to the problems and obstacles which you yourself have decided upon. Before you come you set up your problems in very much the same manner as a chess problem is set up and then left for someone else to solve.

So you have your problems set up in front of you, and instead of just sitting down and scratching your head, and anywhere else which is troubling you at that moment, and trying to work it out, you do something about it. You look about and find the family, the country, the locality which will best enable you to live the problems which you have set up and solve them by the mere act of your living and enduring the difficulties and tests.

After all, a student perhaps going to a post-graduate course, he knows he is going to have some hardships, he knows he has to get a certain percentage of marks otherwise he won't pass, otherwise he's got to come back again. He knows that he'll have to 'serve' a certain time in the classrooms, but he knows all these things and he wants to go through it because he wants the qualifications or the knowledge that comes after. So *you* planned everything, but none of your plans ever included suicide. If you commit suicide, then it means you are a drop-out, it means you failed, and if a person is a drop-out it means he can't advance through lack of qualification and through lack of intestinal fortitude. Always without any exception those who drop out of life through suicide come back and start all over again with a fresh bunch of problems just tagged on for luck.

Next time you look in some newspaper or in some magazine, and you see a chess problem all set up so nicely on the black and white squares of print, well just remember *you* set up problems like that for yourself before you came to this Earth.

How are you solving them? Are you making out all right? Do not be disheartened, you started it, you know!

CHAPTER FIVE

A hundred men may make a camp;
it takes a woman to make a home.

'Tsk, tsk,' said the Old Man to Miss Cleo who was sitting admiring the sunshine coming in through a parting of the curtains. She turned her head wisely and gazed through those beautiful blue eyes. 'Tsk, tsk,' he repeated as if enjoying the sound. 'I wish I were a rich author,' he said, 'and had an extensive reference library. Do you know how many books I have, Clee?' The Old Man turned his head and looked at the only books he possessed, a dictionary, a diabetics' manual, a medical handbook for ships' captains, a book about countries' flags, a Payette catalogue about radio stuff from Montreal, a Canadian tyre catalogue from Toronto, and, of course, a very large atlas, so large that it just about takes two men and a dog to lift the thing, it's certainly an atlas too large and too heavy for a poor wretch confined to bed. 'And that's all this author's library, Clee,' said the Old Man with that wry laugh. 'Rather a pity, though, because the number of things people ask, well, it would be enough to make my hair stand on end if I weren't bald. Still, this is wasting time, we have to get on with our book, Miss Clee, and you and Taddy can go and enjoy the sunshine while I work for the daily bread.'

Mrs. Sorock – our old friend Valeria Sorock – asks about sleep. Good gracious me, Mrs. Sorock, don't you know what sleep is? Anyway, quite a number of people have asked the same thing so let's see what we can do about it.

On the physical plane a body works and builds up a lot of toxins, a lot of poisons accumulate in the muscles. When we work too hard at a given task using the same muscles, crystals form in the muscular tissue and, being wretchedly sharp things, they dig in when we continue moving and make us feel 'stiff', so we soon stop moving.

All the organs of the body get suffused with toxins and so after a time it is necessary for Man to lie down and go to sleep so that the body mechanism slows down, becomes almost static, and during that period of sleep the toxins which cause tiredness and muscular stiffness, dissipate or disperse so that when we wake up we are as good as new. All the stiffness has gone, all the aches and pains have gone, and people feel very refreshed, at least they do if they go to bed early enough and get enough rest, otherwise if people have been out drinking they have overloaded the body mechanism badly and they suffer from a hangover. But we are not discussing drunks and their ilk, we are discussing *your* attitude towards sleep, you, the sensible people.

So on the ordinary physical plane, when we sleep it is with the purpose of dissipating toxins and crystals which make one sluggish, tired, and full of aches and pains.

But there is more to sleep than this. Just as school children go home at the end of the school day, so does the human psyche have to go home at frequent intervals.

If a human had to stay completely awake all the time he would find life insupportable, all manner of strange physical manifestations would occur. So he goes into a period of sleep to the astral world for recuperation. Think of school children who had to stay in class for twenty-four hours a day; well, of course, they couldn't do it, but supposing they had to, soon they would be able to learn anything, soon they would be completely insane with fatigue. The same with adults.

During sleep the physical body is left prone upon a bed, most times it's upon a bed, anyhow, enough times in fact for us to say 'prone upon a bed'. At such times the physical body is resting there and just sleeping off the effects of existing for yet another day. The driver of the body, the psyche, is away

71

so the body mechanism called the sub-conscious takes over, and all sorts of reflex actions occur in the body. Often the eyes will roll behind shut eyelids, often the body will gasp and groan or snort, and there is much threshing about because the body exercises a certain amount during sleep in order that crystals and toxins may be dispersed and dissipated more rapidly. That is why people are moving quite a lot when they are asleep, and no one ever stays completely immobile during sleep. If they did they would have a fresh load of toxins at the point of contact between the body and the bed because all the time the same flesh would be compressed.

The sub-conscious during this sleep period is completely freed from the control of the psyche, and so it, in effect, wanders among the memory-file cards something like an idiot boy who can grasp a file card here, or perhaps two or three file cards there.

If one card only is picked – and remember that we should have put 'card' in quotes to show that it's not really a card, but we are just using a symbolic item. If you like, we could, to make it clearer say that a memory cluster is tapped – if that memory cluster, then, is tapped we get a dream which can be quite clear about one specific event. But if two or three memory clusters (let's call them cards and have done with it!) are picked, then the dream becomes a fantasy because, purely as an illustration, we can have a dream or adventure in which a fish is riding down the road on horseback because the memory picked up may have been of a big fish, and then superimposed upon it will be the memory of a person on horseback. If these two memory cards are superimposed, then we get the distorted impression of a fish on horseback.

If you go in for slide projection with 35 mm transparencies you will know that you can get a very clear picture by having just one slide in your projector, but if you stick in two slides then you get something which never happened, you get one picture superimposed on the other. And if you get three slides in, well, then you get confusion. It's the same with your dreams, the dream is a simple thing, just an ordinary straight-forward memory, but when it becomes tinged or overpowered with a different memory card, then you get fantasy or even nightmare. You dream of things which are quite impossible, things which could never happen, and then if you have retained any control of your memory when your psyche returns to the body, you will say that you had a nightmare.

During sleep when the psyche is away the built-in censor of the body also is sleeping, and so some of the memories or fantasies may be erotic or sadistic, and so we get those terrible dreams of which people sometimes write in and say, 'Chee! Whatever happened to me?'

It is impossible to confuse astral travel with dreams or nightmares because in dreams there is nearly always some inconsistency, come improbability, there in always some element which is at variance with what you know to be fact. The colours may be wrong, or you may, for example, see a person with the head of a tiger. It can be determined, with a little practice, that which is a dream and that which is astral travel.

Memories of dreams and memories of astral travel follow the same path into one's awareness when one is awake; when the psyche comes back and the body awakens it may say, 'Oh, I had a terrible dream last night.' Or if the person has training and knows how to astral travel consciously, then he comes back with a complete knowledge of all he has done. The body is still rested, the toxins are still dispersed, but the *psyche* has retained the information of what happened in the astral world.

Some school children have a holiday and they are so excited at coming back to school that everything that happened during the holiday completely disappears from their brains or from their memories, and in just the same way

73

people coming back from astral travel may forget completely all that happened in the excitement of starting another day.

It cannot be too often repeated that if one wants to remember astral travel, then one just simply must say to oneself three times before going to sleep, 'I will sleep soundly and restfully, and in the morning I will be aware of all that I have done in the astral.' Repeat that three times before going to sleep, and if you really think what you are saying, and if you really mean what you are saying, then you will remember when you awaken. There is nothing magical about it, it's just getting through to a rather stupid subconscious and saying, in effect, 'Hey Bud, you've got to keep alert tonight, no playing about and gumming up the works with my memories, you keep out of the way ready for a fresh load of memories when I return.'

Of course the person who is trained in astral travel can astral travel when he is fully awake. It is quite usual for the trained person to sit down in a chair, clasp his hands and put his feet close together and then just close his eyes. He can then will himself to leave the body and go anywhere and stay fully conscious during the whole period of astral travel so that when the astral body rejoins the physical body there is brought back a completely retained memory of all that happened.

That takes practice, of course, and a bit of self-discipline, it is not difficult to train oneself to remember all that happened when the body is asleep. You just have to tell your sub-conscious to shut up exactly as you tell an unruly schoolboy to shut up. The first telling is more or less a waste of time, at the second telling the sub-conscious jumps to awareness, and with the third telling it is hoped that the command sinks in and the sub-conscious will obey. But if you do this for a few nights you will find that the sub-conscious does obey.

Many people like to keep a notebook and pencil by the

74

bedside so that immediately upon awakening in the morning the knowledge of what happened in the night can be written down, otherwise with the press and turmoil of modern living there is a great tendency to forget what happened. A poor fellow will awaken, for example, and think he is going to be late for work, and then next he will wonder if his wife is in a good temper and will get his breakfast or if he will have to go without. So with things like that on his mind he is not much in a mood to remember what happened in the night. So make a definite practice, keep a notebook and pencil by your bedside and the very first thing you do when you awaken, write down *immediately* everything you remember of the night. With practice you will find it's easy and with a bit more practice you won't need your notebook and your pencil, you will carry out your days on Earth with much more contentment knowing that this is just a hard school and nothing more, knowing that at the end of the school term you will be able to return Home.

Of late there seems to have been a rash of advertisements from all sorts of firms who purport to teach one sleep learning. They want to sell one expensive gizmos and even more expensive taped courses complete with time switch, headphones, under-the-pillow speaker, and what-have-you.

Now it is quite impossible for anyone to learn anything worthwhile while asleep. To start with the driver of the body is away, and all that is left is a sort or crummy caretaker called 'Sub-conscious', and very extensive researches in the leading countries of the world have proved beyond doubt that sleep learning is not possible, it doesn't work.

If you stay awake, that is, if you are slow in going to sleep, then you may pick up a few snatches of conversation from the tapes. But there is no easy way of learning, you can't press a button and say, 'Hey presto' to a machine, because that will not make you a genius overnight. Instead it will interrupt your sleep rhythm and make you a bad tempered, unmentionable you-know-what.

Suppose you leave your car in the garage while you go in your house to have your buttered beans on toast, or whatever it is that you have before going to bed. Well, you would be quite a bit of an optimist in thinking your car was going to learn through tapes while you were away from it. The car manufacturers admittedly make several lurid and impossible claims for their mechanized tin boxes (no, I do not have a car), but even the most optimistic of car advertisers would balk at saying their cars would learn during the owner's sleep.

Your body is just a vehicle, a vehicle whereby your Overself can gain some experience on Earth and on a few other assorted planets, so don't give yourself a lot of airs about how clever you are, how important you are, and all that, because when it comes down to brass tacks or whatever standard of value you want to use, 'you' are just a lump of protoplasm which is driven around by day by an owner who happens to be your Overself. You can liken it to the Irishman and his donkey; the donkey stays in the stable by night, but no amount of tapes will enable the donkey to speak English or even American, yet during the day the owner can be taught to learn – even American. It might be worth trying to teach an Irishman Welsh one day to see if that can be done.

I think actually I deserve a medal for pointing out to you some of these things which are designed to take your hard-earned money from you. Always think, what's behind the advertisement? Well, obviously, the advertiser wants to get your money. It reminds me of the people who advertise how to make a million in, say, three easy lessons, or how to forecast the Irish Sweepstake and win the first prize. If these people who could do such things did them, then they wouldn't bother to advertise, would they? And if they can't do it, well, they have to make money in some other way, by pretending that they can make millions in a month. They can if enough people reply to their advertisements, but don't you be one of them, button up your pocket, keep your handbag shut, keep your mouth shut too, and your ears wide open.

Oh Glory Be, and all the rest of it, now here's a question – you'd better get ready to read this carefully. 'You say the sub-conscious is stupid, yet in "Chapters of Life" it is said to be very, very intelligent, it seems to be more intelligent than the part of us you say is one-tenth conscious. Now, tell us straight out, is it stupid or is it super-intelligent?'

If we are going down into basics again, like this, then we have to say that the sub-conscious is neither intelligent nor unintelligent because it doesn't have intelligence, it's a different sort of thing altogether. The sub-conscious is just a repository of knowledge, good knowledge, bad knowledge. It's just a filing system. It contains all you have ever heard, all you have ever seen, all you have ever experienced. It reminds your automatic responses when to breathe in and when to breathe out. It reminds part of you to wriggle and screech if you are tickled, etc. It's just an automatic reminder.

Would you say that a librarian is intelligent? Well, that's a matter of opinion, of course. I know I tried to deal with those silly librarians at a famous Library in London, the ones who put down details, and I tried to tell these people that the details they were putting down about me were utterly and incontrovertibly incorrect, but it's such a job convincing some of them, and I am left with the indelible opinion that the Record Library librarians at that famous Library are not intelligent. Anyway, that's a matter of opinion, but let us make that query again just for the sake of answering this question :–

Would you consider that a librarian was a genius? Would you consider that a librarian could answer any question about anything and say what any person has said before? Well, of course you couldn't, not even if you were a librarian yourself could you make such claims. Instead you would say, quite correctly, that – no, there is no such knowledge in a conscious human, but a librarian knows where to find certain information. The best librarians are those who can find the information fastest.

You and I could go to a library and fumble our way through certain filing cabinets in search of a book title containing matter on the subject of interest. Then we would find we had to refer to something else, then we would find that the book was out of print or out of circulation or out of the Library. We would waste half a day or more, yet by asking a librarian there is a second during which he has an absolutely blank expression, and then the penny seems to drop with a clank, and he or she gets into motion and produces the book with the desired information.

If he or she is good at the work, they recommend many more books.

The sub-conscious is like that. As soon as the thinking 'we' desires to know something, then the sub-conscious tries to come up with the answer. That is not intelligence, that is entirely automatic, and as it's automatic it can be trained.

Trained for what? Well, the answer is simple. Your sub-conscious is your memory. If you have a poor memory it means that your conscious one-tenth is not getting through to your sub-conscious nine-tenths. If you have a poor memory it means that the sub-conscious is falling down on the job of providing you the information which you demand.

Supposing you want to know what Gladstone really said back in the year 18-something-or-other. Well, you've probably heard it, you've probably read of it, so it's in your memory and if your sub-conscious cannot bring it out it means that there is a fault in a relay somewhere.

Some people can reel off a terrible lot of stuff about football or baseball teams, and give all the winners or whatever they are called for years back, but that is because they are interested in the subject, and people cannot remember things in which they are not interested. Never having seen a football match or a baseball match, and not wanting to, I haven't the vaguest idea about it. I thought that a baseball diamond, for instance, was a thing given to prize winners; no doubt somebody will write in to tell me differently.

If you want to cultivate a good memory, then you have to cultivate your sub-conscious. You have to be interested in a subject, until you are interested the sub-conscious cannot 'tag on.' Many of our lady readers will know all about the male film star, how many times he has been married, how many times he has been divorced, and how many times he has chased his beloved-for-the-moment around the world. That's easy, they can do that, but just ask them to go and get a standard fine thread from a local shop, perhaps a three-sixteenth standard fine thread, and they'll come back looking blanker than usual.

To train your memory, that is, to train your sub-conscious, you should think clearly about things and assume an interest in those things. If men are sent shopping for women's things, well, they come back without a single thought in their heads, but if they took an interest in things then their memory would improve. One can take an interest by asking oneself why a woman wants this, or that, or something else, and the woman can ask herself why a man should want, for instance, a three-sixteenth bolt of fine thread. If she can get a definite interest, then he or she can remember.

If you are trying to remember something specific such as a telephone number, then try to imagine the person to whom the telephone number belongs, or if you do not know the person or cannot visualize him or her, then look at the telephone number – is it a series of circles or a lot of strokes? For example, 6's, 9's, o's become circles, as do 3's and 2's. But strokes would be 1's, 7's, etc. – and, of course, 4's. So if you can visualize a number by circles or strokes, you can remember it. The best way is to use our old system of threes. Repeat the telephone number three times while holding the sincere conviction that you will always remember that number. You can, you know, it's quite easy, nothing difficult in it.

79

Another thing which can be done during the period of sleep is to approach another person whom one desires to influence. Now, sleep learning is useless, that is absolutely a waste of time because you are trying to teach the body something when the entity that controls the body is out of the body. But let us deal with something else – influencing others.

Supposing that Mr. John Brown very much desires to get an appointment with the firm of the XYZ Manufacturing Company. Mr. Brown has heard that this Company is an extremely good company and that it is definitely desirable to be employed by such a firm.

Mr. Brown has had some good fortune in getting an appointment with the personnel manager or someone else in authority for, say, the following day. Now, if Mr. Brown really wants to sell himself, this is what he will do:–

He will get hold of any information he can about the firm and especially about the person with whom he has the interview. That means that Mr. Brown must make a definite inquiry as to who will do the interviewing. Then if it is at all possible he will get a photograph of the interviewer, and before going to bed that night Mr. Brown will sit quite alone and he will visualize himself talking to the interviewer on the morrow. Mr. Brown will convincingly state (in the privacy of his bedroom) the reasons why he would be a desirable employee, the reasons why he needs that particular appointment, the reasons why he considers he is worth more than the firm normally pays. He says all this to the photograph, then he lifts up his feet and tucks them in bed, and he puts the photograph so that it is facing him as he lies on his accustomed side.

Mr. Brown goes to sleep with the firm, very definite, very emphatic intention of getting out of his body and journeying to Mr. Interviewer's house. There he will meet Mr. Interviewer out of his body, and Mr. Brown's astral will tell Mr. Interviewer's astral all that Mr. Brown has just said in the privacy of his bedroom.

Fantastic? Daft? Don't you believe it! This really works. If the Interviewee (I hope that is right; it means the one who is going to be interviewed) plays his cards properly, then the interviewer will give him the job. That is sure, that is definite, it really works.

Now, you who want a better job or more money, go through those words again and put them into practice. You can influence people in this way, but not necessarily for bad. You cannot influence a person to do that which he or she would not normally do, that is, you cannot influence a person to do an evil or wrong act, which means that some of you fellows who write in to me asking how to get power over girls – well, you can't friend, you can't, and don't try.

Yes, innocent readers, ladies of high degree and of the utmost purity, I sometimes get letters from 'gentlemen' who ask me to teach them to hypnotize girls or to put spells on girls or to produce the formula of something which will render girls helpless so that the 'gentleman' – well, what would he do under such circumstances? Anyway, I tell them the truth which is that unless they go in for poisoning they cannot influence another person to do that which the other person's conscience would not normally permit. So there you are. If your desires are pure or 'clean', then you can influence others, you can influence others to do good but not to do bad. Most people don't need influencing to do bad anyhow, it seems to come natural.

It might be as well here to introduce a question having bearing on some of the remarks made in previous chapters. The question is:–

'You say that people come to this Earth time after time until the person concerned does his specific task. You also say that at times groups of people come for the same purpose. Can you give any definite illustration on that point?'

As a matter of fact – yes, quite definitely, yes. Now, I had a cutting some time ago in the Spanish language, and this Spanish language thing gave a lot of details about a magazine called *Excalibur* which had been published some years ago, apparently, in Durban, South Africa. I have only a very, very brief comment on the whole matter, but it seems the magazine published some remarkable proven parallels between the life and death of President Lincoln of the U.S.A. and President Kennedy of the U.S.A. This will so adequately reply to many querents that I will give all the details here. Let us do them numerically as then it will be so much easier if you want to refer to them or discuss them with your friends. So here the first one is :–

1. President Lincoln was elected to that Office in the year 1860. That, of course, can be ascertained from history books. So – Lincoln became President in 1860, and here is the first coincidence; Kennedy became President in 1960, a hundred years later.

2. It might shake you to know that President Lincoln was assassinated on a Friday. President Kennedy was assassinated on a Friday.

3. You may have read that President Lincoln was at a theatre enjoying a stage show in the presence of his wife, and he was then assassinated in the presence of his wife. President Kennedy was visiting Dallas, Texas, and he was riding in a car with his wife. He also was enjoying the show, that is, the show of public acclaim, etc.

4. President Lincoln was shot in the back while sitting in a box at the theatre. President Kennedy was shot in the back while sitting in a car.

5. President Lincoln was succeeded by a man called Johnson. Johnson became President after President Lincoln, but in Texas President Kennedy was killed and Vice-President Johnson was sworn in as President of the U.S.A. on board an aircraft bringing the body of the late President and the living new President back to the capital.

6. But we have not finished with our list of coincidences, yet, not by a long way. The Johnson who succeeded President Lincoln was a Democrat from South U.S.A., and Lyndon Johnson who succeeded President Kennedy also is a Democrat from the South – from Texas. So that is quite a

good list of 'coincidences', isn't it: Though to show that there is more than chance taking a part in things, enough to show that there must be some 'Divine Plan' making the entity who was President Lincoln perhaps come back as Kennedy so that a task could be accomplished.

All right, let's get back with—

7. Both the Johnsons had been members of the Senate before becoming President.

8. Lincoln's successor was Andrew Johnson. Now really read this ... Andrew Johnson was born in 1808, but the Johnson who succeeded President Kennedy was born in 1908.

9. Lincoln was assassinated by a rather strange sort of a person, a thoroughly dissatisfied sort of person if we are to believe the report, which is now history, and that assassin of Lincoln was John Wilkes Booth and he was born in 1839. Lee Harvey Oswald who, it was stated, murdered President Kennedy appears also to have been a very dissatisfied sort of person, one who had been in trouble all too frequently. He was born in 1939.

10. To continue with our list of 'coincidences', Booth was assassinated before he could be brought to trial, but so was Oswald; Oswald was shot while being moved by the Police, and before he could be brought to trial.

11. These coincidences, as you have seen, extend not only to the Presidents and the assassins, but also to the wives of the Presidents because Mrs. Lincoln, the wife of President Lincoln, lost a child while in the White House, and Mrs. Kennedy, the wife of President Kennedy, lost a child while in the White House.

12. Lincoln had a Secretary and that Secretary was called Kennedy. Secretary Kennedy advised President Lincoln most strongly not to go to the theatre where he was assassinated. President Kennedy had a Secretary also and he was called Lincoln, and Secretary Lincoln strongly advised President Kennedy not to go to Dallas!

13. John Wilkes Booth shot President Lincoln in the back

while the President was watching a show and then the assassin, Booth ran to hide in a store. But Lee Harvey Oswald
shot at Kennedy from a store and ran to hide in a theatre.
You just read that carefully again and see how very strange
it is. One assassin shot in a theatre and hid in a store, the
other one shot from a store and hid in a theatre.

14. L-I-N-C-O-L-N is seven letters, and if you count up
K-E-N-N-E-D-Y you will find that that also has seven
letters.

15. If you count John Wilks Booth you will find that there
are fifteen letters, and if you count Lee Harvey Oswald you
will find that that has fifteen letters.

16. It is believed that Oswald killed Kennedy and Oswald
had accomplices. None of this has been actually, definitely,
incontrovertibly proved; it is a matter of circumstantial evi-
dence, no one can prove that Booth murdered Lincoln. In
the same way Oswald, it was stated, had accomplices, but it
has not been conclusively proved that Oswald did murder
Kennedy, and it has not been proved that Oswald had accomplices. Let's face it quite bluntly — circumstantial evi-
dence points clearly at Booth and at Oswald, but again how
much of what we could read was actual truth and how much
was the press pre-judging and pre-condemning a man? We
do not know and I point out this because it is another coincidence in the case of two men.

17. You will remember that the man called Ruby, who
was a bit of a fanatic, killed Oswald, he shot Oswald in front
of the television cameras, he just pushed his way past the
police, pointed a gun and pulled a trigger. But Boston Corbett was also a bit of a fanatic, he too believed that he was
doing right when he murdered John Wilkes Booth. In both
cases these two men killed the man suspected and accused of
the murder of a President, and in both cases it was stated
that the second assassin, that is Corbett and Ruby, did so out
of excessive loyalty for the President of the time. But in
neither case is the actual motive established.

In another book I wrote about the Overself managing a group of puppets. Well, you think about that in the light of this information, where two Presidents were elected a hundred years apart, they were both assassinated on a Friday, and – look through the list again and see all the different coincidences. Now, do you seriously believe that these could be just coincidences? It isn't really possible, you know. My own belief is that Lincoln did not do his job, and so he had to come back to substantially the same job to finish what he did not do before.

The only way to come back was to come back as one who would be President of the U.S.A. which is what he did. You can take it that sometimes an Overself has 'dress rehearsals' with puppets, so in the case of Lincoln the stage was set, appropriately enough at a theatre, and a President was assassinated. Nothing was proved against the assumed murderer and the assumed murderer was assassinated by another person. It was all most unsatisfactory, motives were unknown and nothing was ever proved against anyone, so perhaps the Overself got a bit fed up with such a waste of time and effort and another arrangement was made for a hundred years later because in the astral world time is different from here, you know. The Other Side of death the astral could have sat down and scratched his metaphorical head, so to speak, and wondered what to do next. Well, by the time he had fidgeted around and scratched a bit more, a hundred years by Earth time would be slipping by.

One also wonders what happens now, was that Overself satisfied with the second attempt, or will there be a third? Personally I believe that we shall yet see a President of the U.S.A. who is actually put in seclusion for being insane. Now I know all the old jokes about Presidents of the U.S.A. being mad in any case, and far be it from me to discourage them, but this time it is a serious matter, and I believe that before too long we shall see a President of the U.S.A. who has to be relieved of his duties because he is too insane to continue. I also believe that we shall see another very difficult thing; I believe that we shall see many most important and influential members of the U.S. Government indicted for Communist activities – for giving aid and comfort to the enemy and for selling out their own country. Some of you who are fairly young will see all that because it is going to happen. There are going to be some truly horrendous things happening to the U.S.A. So keep your radios switched on in the next few years!

CHAPTER SIX

Time is the most valuable thing a
man can spend.

THE Old Man was in his new bed, the new hospital bed with the motor which lifted the head-piece up and down and which, by pressing a button, adjusted the height of the bed. Up and down he went playing with the thing somewhat like a child with a new toy, perhaps, but it's not so easy when one cannot get about at all, when one has to lie in bed, a bed which is so low that one is prevented from even looking out of the window. Now the Old Man had a bed, the height of which could be adjusted by an electric motor. He thought of himself as a submarine surfacing for a look at the world.

'Hey!' yelled Miss Cleopatra, 'how the heck do you think we are going to jump on the bed if you keep altering the height like that, how do you think we can judge our distance?'

The Old Man came back to the present with quite a jerk, and hastily set the bed to go its lowest. Miss Cleopatra jumped up and stood on the Old Man's chest full of indignation. 'You trying to get rid of me?' she asked. 'Do you want to make it difficult, so I can't come and stand on your chest, hey?'

'No, of course not, Cleo,' replied the Old Man, 'but just think, if you stand up here on my chest you can look over that stupid balcony outside our window and you can see the ships in the harbour.'

Together they lay there looking out over the harbour. Closest was a ship unloading nickel ore, beyond that was a Russian ship very deep in the water astern but with the bows well out showing that all the forepart had yet to be loaded. A little farther, two berths farther on, actually, a South Korean ship was loading wood pulp for Korea. 'Don't know why they want to come here for wood pulp,' said the Old Man, 'there's plenty of trees in South Korea.'

'Oh well,' said Buttercup, 'probably they want to do a barter or something, and they want to buy woodpulp from Canada in exchange for something else.'

Buttercup was definitely the expert when it came to ships and shipping, Buttercup was a specialist when it came to ship's flags. The unusual South Korean flag defeated her for just a few moments, but – anything else, Panama, Monrovia, even the old Red Ensign, she could distinguish it miles off!

Miss Taddy looked up, 'What *are* you doing, Guv?' she asked in a rather puzzled fashion. 'Have you got so sick that you are talking to yourself?'

'No, of course I'm not talking to myself, I'm just making some notes for a book. Can't I make some notes, can't I speak without you interfering, Taddykins?'

Taddykins shook her head in puzzled amazement and then curled up in a nice compact ball and dropped off to sleep again. Suddenly Miss Cleo's ears pricked up and Taddy jerked to full awareness. Outside a strident voice came, 'Well, I looked in the papers today and I saw my horoscope wasn't so good so I thought, well, I thought to myself, if you didn't have a job to do, Old Girl, you'd be better staying off and being in bed, but you can't do that when you gotter earn a living, when you gotter man to keep, can you?' The voice passed on accompanied by the mumble of some other woman, probably belching out some drivel about her own troubles.

'Ah yes,' said the Old Man, 'that reminds me, that's a question which I had here. Let's see, where is it?' He riffled through a pile of letters and triumphantly came up with the desired one.

Postmark, well somewhere in one of the far Islands; subject, what is it? 'Dear Sir, I enclose a dollar and my birthdate. Please send me a full horoscope and life reading immediately, and send it to me by return by airmail. If there is any change keep it for someone who didn't send a postal charge.'

Now, what do you think of that? Someone thinks that horoscopes grow on trees. They are not so easy as that, it takes time. But here is another question:

'What do you really think of horoscopes? Do all these people who advertise do it for a racket? A horoscope has never been right for me. What's the truth of it all?'

Well, the truth of astrology is this; given the right conditions, astrology can be completely accurate and successful ... given the right conditions.

Let me first of all warn you against all this run-of-the-mill advertising offering to do your horoscope for a couple of dollars or a few shillings. What you get is a few printed pieces of paper which purport to be a horoscope, but that stuff is hardly worth putting out for garbage, and in my considered opinion the same can be said for all this rot which is alleged to come from computers, it just isn't worth the money. Astrology is not just a mechanical process. Astrology is a science and an art, one cannot do it altogether by science, art is necessary, and one cannot do it altogether by art because science is necessary.

To do a horoscope properly – really accurately, that is – it is necessary to have the precise time of birth and the actual location of birth. Then it is necessary to spend many days working out various aspects, etc. It cannot be done successfully for five or ten dollars, what you get from that sort of thing is just a rough, very rough, guide, which can apply to thousands of different people. I will not do a horoscope for anyone for any price because I do not believe in people having their horoscopes done. If people have a horoscope done they feel that they just have to do everything the horoscope says, and a horoscope is not an absolutely cast iron set of conditions. A horoscope is a set of possibilities. By knowing a person's astrological make-up one can describe what the person's appearance should be like, one can describe what the person's character should be like, and the horoscope sets the limits of what the person can be. For example, one person can have a certain horoscope which says that he cannot rise above the station to which he was born, but that he can do certain things with immense effort.

The second person could have a horoscope which says that he will rise above his station and he will progress very rapidly with hardly any effort at all. If you really want to know what the horoscope is like consider it in this light; it is a specification, an informed guess of what a person's capabilities are.

To make it clearer let us take two cars. The 'horoscope' of a Rolls-Royce car can say that the car will be very silent, very fast, very comfortable, that it will have a certain maximum speed and it will use so much petrol every few miles. The horoscope of the second car perhaps – are there still Morris Minor's in England? – will say that it is a low-powered car, very very suitable for local jaunts, that its maximum speed is such-and-such a figure, that it doesn't use much petrol, and it is a very nice little car for getting about in traffic. Well, people are like that, they have their specifications only we call them horoscopes.

A horoscope will not tell the eager young lady, you know, the one who is anxious to get a husband in a hurry, that she will go out and meet 'Mr. Right' under the third lamp-post as she turns to the left or to the right, or that she will meet a dark haired young man who is busy tying his shoe laces, and it will be love at first sight. That's not horoscopes at all, that's not real astrology, that is fake fortune-telling.

There are very very few really genuine, really capable astrologers advertising. They don't have to advertise. Their fame, their accuracy, is passed by word of mouth, and if you think you can fill in a coupon and send it off with fifty cents or five shillings and get a life reading – well, think again, for you are one of the gullible ones who really deserve to be caught in the sucker trap for thinking you can get something so cheaply. You only get what you pay for.

I will not do horoscopes for any sum of money. If I do them I do them free under very special circumstances, but in my considered opinion no horoscope which costs less than a hundred dollars is worth having because it means that the person who did the horoscope just did not spend enough time and take enough trouble, so all you have is just a few marks on a piece of paper.

In my own case my past was foretold by astrology with utterly stupendous accuracy. Everything that was foretold about me has happened, sadly enough a few things extra have happened, a few things which the astrologer didn't get around to discussing, and all the wretched 'extras' were bad things, too!

To answer a question, then, 'Is astrology genuine?' I will say, yes, astrology can be very genuine, it can suggest what a person's life will be like, it can indicate probabilities, but they are probabilities only. So do not take astrology too seriously unless you get an absolute gem of an astrologer who knows exactly what he is doing and who is completely ethical, that is, one who tells you the truth, the whole truth, and nothing but the truth. So many people, so many astrologers, have their 'information' and put in quite a few stock paragraphs because they know what people want to hear.

Now here is another one, 'My daughter's husband is a very strange sort of man, he doesn't believe in the same things as those in which I believe, he doesn't believe in occult things. What can I do to make him?'

The only answer that one can give here is to state most definitely that nothing can be done to help in the way in which the lady means. If a person is not yet ready to study occult subjects then it is definitely wrong to try to force occult things at him.

Everyone has a right to free choice, and whichever choice they make is entirely their own affair, and their own responsibility. If Billy Bugsbottom decides that 'occult stuff is all a lot of hogwash', then why should one try to persuade Billy Bugsbottom anything different, it's his belief and his choice, and it is definitely wrong to influence a person.

There are so many people who write in asking how they can do a Mantra to compel some pour wretch to do something which they just would hate to do, and I repeat *ad nauseum* that it is wrong to influence another person. Perhaps the person has some definite reason for not wanting to study astrology or occultism or how to play snakes and ladders. In the same way it is quite wrong to expect a person to agree with us in everything we do. You should hear how Buttercup and I agree to differ. There are many things which I know from actual experience to be fact, but Buttercup is entitled to her own opinion and if my beliefs are not always her beliefs, that is her choice and I do not influence her at all. The crummy press often print articles saying that Buttercup is a disciple of mine; they couldn't be farther from the truth! She is not a disciple of mine, nor is she a Buddhist. To start with I have no disciples and never had any, and secondly I believe it is wrong for people to switch sides and become a Buddhist when they really want to be a Christian, or a Christian when they really want to be a Buddhist. Being a bit biased on the matter, I always say that when a person is ready they will become a Buddhist automatically because the real Buddhism just means obeying the law of doing unto others as you would have them do unto you. Of course I am not meaning some of these peculiar cults in England and in the U.S.A. who now call themselves Buddhist 'temples'. That is not my idea of Buddhism at all. The real Buddhist doesn't have to go out and get converts. I am a real Buddhist.

While on the subject of astrology, because we are, more or less, let us have a look at two other systems. Now, graphology, which is the science of reading character from handwriting, is a thing which I thoroughly endorse when done by an expert. Graphology is not fortune-telling, it is instead a most accurate method of determining a person's character, potentialities, and all the rest of it. Of course one has to be an expert at such things. Too many beginners or outright fakes base their conclusions on just one or two points in the handwriting, but one has to have about seven confirmations before one can say with absolute certainty, without any fear of contradiction at all, that this is so or that is so.

Handwriting tells character and ability and all that. It is not in any way possible to forecast the future from handwriting and no reputable graphologist ever claims that it is. The ideal use for graphology is in assessing a person's ability for a certain job.

Some years ago 'Ma', to whom we now refer as 'Ra'ab', did graphology for certain industrial firms, and she did it successfully. Firms would supply her with the handwriting of people who applied to the firm for employment, and then Ra'ab would quite accurately suggest which applicant was the most suitable and give an assessment of his character and abilities.

Oh, by the way, perhaps I should say how 'Ma' has suddenly become 'Ra'ab'; well, the cats thought that the first name (Ma) would remind people too much of Dinah Dripdry's Ma, the charlady, and so we used instead a name which she used in a previous life, Ra'ab. That is one of my infamous digressions, by the way, never mind, it's better to have a digression than no book, or don't you think so?

In this particular book there are going to be many digressions and there are going to be many repetitions; I have been looking through a whole series of questions, and I see that it is quite essential to have repetitions even if one or two of you do not like it. So you are being warned now that there will be a few repetitions. I can safely warn you now that you are so far into the book and, I hope, have bought the book instead of borrowing it from some library. A poor wretched author doesn't get any royalties on books supplied to a Library, you know, and every book read from the Library shelves is a loss of income, that is, a loss of food, to the author. People write to me and tell me that they have read part of one of my books in a Public Library and now would I please tell them the answers to a lot of questions, or, if I will send them a complete set of my books, each autographed and with a photograph of me, they will try to find time to read the books. Hopeful little souls, aren't they? So – now that you've got so far and presumably have bought this book let me say that, yes, there are going to be a few repetitions but it's all in a good cause. I hope repetition will enable you to get all this in your sub-conscious. You had to practise repetition before you could do the multiplication tables, and I am trying to do something for you, help you by placing this knowledge into your sub-conscious.

There are many firms who choose applicants largely on the basis of the handwriting, and so it's to your own interest to brush up on your handwriting. You might get a better job or more money that way. You might also get an assessment of character from a good graphologist because that will help you to overcome any weakness in character and to strengthen those which are already strong. But never, never believe that you can have your 'fortune' told from your handwriting. You cannot.

One of the original systems for telling a person's past, present and future is by palmistry, reading all those queer marks on the palm. Again, if one really knows how to do it it is just about infallible. In brief and assuming that you are right handed, then your left hand will indicate what you planned to do in this life, and will indicate the equipment with which you came, that is, are you artistic, are you a plodder, are you quick tempered or stolid? The left hand tells what one planned, but the right hand shows what one has actually achieved up to date. The average practitioner can give quite a good assessment of character from the lines of the hands and fingers, but it needs to be a far more than average practitioner to be able to tell truthfully of the past life and the probabilities for the future. Now, let me stress that point again; the 'probabilities.' There is nothing on this Earth that can say definitely and incontrovertibly what will happen to a person, there is no science, no art, no skill, no device which will say what is going to happen to a person beyond any shadow of doubt. Truthful practitioners will admit that they can tell only probabilities.

Take, by way of example, some poor fellow who falls out of a plane without a parachute; well, anyone would be justified in saying that he is virtually dead as soon as he starts to fall because as soon as he stops falling there is a horrid splat, and he has left his mark on the Earth. But, wait a moment – he may not fall on something hard. There are quite a few cases of people falling out of aeroplanes and surviving to tell the tale – which they do! In my own case I fell out of a plane when it was on fire, I fell about a thousand feet, and I sustained very severe spine injuries which caused a certain amount of curvature of the spine. Other people have fallen safely, there was one poor fellow who fell out of a plane and hit a haystack and his only real danger was the fear of being suffocated before watchers could take him out, dig him out from the bottom of the haystack. He got a bump or two and a king size fright, but he was no worse off.

Another well known case happened in Switzerland. The pilot had to leave his plane and he left without his parachute, it seems, and he fell through the cold Swiss air and landed in a deep snowdrift. His only danger was in freezing to death, and people had to dig frantically to dig him out, and his only trouble was feeling a bit chilly. So you see any astrologer would have said that the fellow would meet his death in an air accident because the probability would be there but the actuality wasn't.

If any soothsayer, clairvoyant, astrologer, palmist, etc., etc., *ad lib*, tells you such a thing will definitely be, then just grab your money and run for it. You can be told probabilities but always, always keep in mind that they are probablities only and nothing more, nothing at all more. If you can keep your head and use a little bit of will-power and imagination, the probabilities can be overcome.

There is a classic example of that. Do you know it? Well,

Socrates, one of the very wise men, had his horoscope prepared, it seems, when he was a very young man. The horoscope indicated that he would be a most enthusiastic thug and murderer and would engage in all forms of villainy with great elan. The young Socrates exclaimed to himself the Greek equivalent of 'Bud, that's for the birds; I'm changing fast,' and decided to do something about it. So he channelled all his energies into knowledge, into philosophical works, and now he is revered as one of the great Sages, he has made his indelible mark on the pages of time whereas if he had just sat down under the weight of an unfavourable horoscope he might have just left his imprint on the Crooks' Calendar of Crime. So there it is, even if an astrologer or a palmist tells you something which frightens you enormously, remember, you can overcome it, you can always sidetrack bad things.

By letters which I receive I gather that most of you have the impression that authors such as I recline in plush splendour and have a whole gang of secretaries waiting with bated breath to hurry to do one's bidding. I gather that many of you think that an author such as I has a Rolls-Royce knocking at the door, ready to take me out. It's not so, it's not so at all. Actually I am reclining in some discomfort in a hospital type bed and, at the moment, through disabilities, etc., I am not able to type, so Buttercup the Benevolent is typing for me as she has typed most of my books – typed them well too, by the way. But do you know what sort of questions I get? Admittedly you know about some of them, but do you know about the questions which I do not normally answer? How would *you*, for example, answer this Question. 'Tell us about such things as casting shadow through standing in sunlight?' Question. 'Is there really such a thing as distance and is the globe really spheroid?' Question. 'What is the meaning of right this and right that? Does that mean one should eat only with the right hand?'

That last question is quite sensible, you know. You might think that some sort of nut or kook sent it in, but if you think about it seriously there is a lot of sense to it. What is the meaning of right this and right that? Well, we know all about doing things the right way and avoiding wrong, we know it is right to do good instead of to do wrong, but do you know that our hands have polarity? One hand is positive and one hand is negative. If you read back a few paragraphs to where we dealt with palms you will see that the left hands deals with the abstract, that is, things before we came to this Earth, how we planned things, whereas the right hand is the practical hand, the hand which says how far we have achieved our objectives.

In the same way some of the Arabs of a few years ago had a very definite ruling about hands. The left hand was known as the 'dirty hand', and that hand could be used only for dirty tasks such as dealing with certain aspects of one's toilet, but the right hand was the 'clean' hand, and one could only use the right hand when dealing with food. All foodstuff was touched with the right hand although one could pick up a cup or a glass with the left hand. It would be quite interesting to investigate the matter further and see how much difference it made to one's digestion when one touched food with the right hand only, and then, perhaps a month later, touch food with the left hand only.

The right hand is the correct hand for holding a dagger or sword, or shaking hands with a person. In the old days people used to carry a knife or dagger in the right hand as a means of warding off attackers, so when they met a friend they would extend the right hand to show that they had no knife hidden, to show that they came in friendship. And so we had the start of the custom of shaking hands – shake a person's hand and you can see that he is not holding a knife against his palm with his thumb, and if he has any weapons concealed in his sleeve – well, shake them out.

From the same source there is another question. It is:

'How does the Silver Cord connect the physical, and the Overself, and the astral at the same time?'

The Silver Cord, like everything else, is a vibration, which means that it is also a source of energy. The Cord does not necessarily have to go to just one other object, that is, it is not limited to connecting body and soul together. Extensions can be taken from it in just the same way as you can have extensions taken from your telephone. If you have a telephone in your living room, then it's no great difficulty to have an extension to your bedroom.

It is ordinary common sense to realize that the Overself is the source of each person's energy, the source of each person's being, and the Overself, you can say, has each human on a leash. So just as you can have a dog on a leash, or you can have ten dogs all on leashes, so you can have an Overself connected to an astral and to a physical body. There is really nothing to answer in that question except to say that if you have a dog, let us say a big dog, at the end of a leash it is quite easy to connect a small dog to the leash of the big dog and that would correspond to the Overself, the astral, and the physical.

Through writing books I have come into contact with some perfectly horrible people, some real 'kooks' who might well be classed as mental home drop-outs. They are in the great minority, but I have also come into contact with some remarkably nice people. For example, there are two very nice ladies in British Columbia, Miss and Mrs. Newman; they are truly trying to make a success of life and I consider that they are achieving success. They have sent some questions and here in this chapter I am going to reply to just one of the questions for the special reason that it fits in so well. So here is an answer to a specific question from Miss and Mrs. Newman. The question is, 'Will you please explain homosexuality in much the same way as you explained alcoholics in "Beyond the Tenth"?'

Our Overself, as I have explained, is getting experience on Earth. The Overself itself is too big, too powerful and too high-vibrating to come to Earth, and so it has to employ those lumps of protoplasm which we in our ignorance think is the highest form of existence anywhere. We humans are just hunks of meat supported on a bony framework and propelled around by grace of the Overself, but inevitably hitch-ups occur.

Sometimes a car manufacturer says to himself (in effect, of course) 'Oh, glory be, I've connected the brakes back-before-frontways on such-and-such a car. Let's call it back.' So notices go out to car owners and the cars have to be recalled to the factory for certain things to be put right.

In the hurly-burly of getting from the astral world to that world we call Earth, mix-ups occur. Being born is a traumatic experience, it's a most violent affair, and a very delicate mechanism can easily become deranged. For example, a baby is about to be born and throughout the pregnancy the mother has been rather careless about what she was eating and what she was doing, so the baby has not received what one might term a balanced chemical input. The baby may be short of a chemical and so development of certain glands may have been halted. Let us say the baby was going to come as a girl, but through lack of certain chemicals, the baby is actually born a boy, a boy with the inclinations of a girl.

The parents might realize that they've got a sissyfied little wretch and put it down to over-indulgence or something, they may try to beat some sense into him one end or the other to make him more manly, but it doesn't work; if the glands are wrong, never mind what sort of attachments are stuck on in front, the boy is still a girl in a boy's body.

At puberty the boy may not develop satisfactorily, or again, he may to all outward appearances. At school he may well appear to be one of the limp-wristed fraternity, but the poor fellow can't help that.

When he reaches man's estate he finds he cannot 'do the things that come naturally', instead he runs after boys — men. Of course he does because all his desires are the desires of a woman. The psyche itself is female, but through an unfortunate set of circumstances the female has been supplied with male equipment, it might not be much use but its still there!

The male then becomes what used to be called a 'pansy' and has homosexual tendencies. The more the psyche is female, the stronger will be the homosexual tendencies.

If a woman has a male psyche, then she will not be interested in men but will be interested in women, because her psyche, which is closer to the Overself than is the physical body, is relaying confusing messages to the Overself and the Overself sends back a sort of command, 'Get busy, do your stuff.' The poor wretched male psyche is obviously repelled by the thought of 'doing his stuff' with a man, and so all the interest is centred on a female, so you get the spectacle of a female making love to a female and that's what we call a lesbian because of a certain island off Greece where that used to be 'the done thing'.

It is quite useless to condemn homosexuals, they are not villains, instead they should be classed as sick people, people who have glandular troubles, and if medicine and doctors had the brains they were born with then they would do something about that glandular defect.

After my own experiences of late I am even more convinced that Western doctors are a crummy lot of kooks just out to make a fast buck. My own experiences have been unmentionably and adjectivally deplorable, however we are not discussing me now, we are discussing homosexuals.

If a lesbian (woman) or a homosexual (male) can find a sympathetic doctor, then glandular extracts can be given which certainly improve the condition a lot and make life bearable, but unfortunately nowadays with the present breed of doctor who seems to be out to make money only, well, you have to search a long way to get a good doctor. But it is useless to condemn a homosexual, it is not his fault or her fault. They are very very unhappy people because they are confused, they don't know what has happened to them, they know that people are sneering at them, and they can't help what is, after all, the strongest impulse known to man or woman – the reproduction impulse.

Head shrinkers alias psychologists are not much help

really because they take years to do what the average person would do in a few days. If it is clearly explained to the homosexuals that they have a glandular imbalance, then they can usually adjust. Anyhow, the laws are being amended to cater for such cases instead of subjecting them to such fierce persecution and imprisonment for what is truly an illness.

There are various ways of helping such people. The first is that a very understanding and much older person who has deep sympathy with the sufferer should explain precisely what has happened. The second is the same as the first but with the addition that the victim should be given some medicament which suppresses the sexual urge, the sexual drive. The third – well, again, matters should be explained, and a qualified doctor can give hormone or testrone injections which can definitely help the body in the matter of sexual adjustment.

The vital thing is that one should never, never condemn a homosexual, it's not his fault, he is being penalized for something he hasn't done, he is being penalized for some fault of Nature; perhaps his mother had the wrong sort of food, perhaps the mother and the child were chemically incompatible. However, whichever way you look at it, homosexuals can only be helped by true understanding and sympathy, and possibly with the judicious administration of drugs.

I see here a question which actually we have already answered. Perhaps I had better answer it again. The question is, 'How did the misconception occur that occultists cannot charge for their services?'

The answer is not far to seek. In the Far East most peoole are desperately poor, they do not have televisions and cars and private aircraft and split level homes. Sometimes they just have food and a few clothes, sometimes people of the Far East do not see money during the whole of their lifetime. Instead they make their purchases by barter, they exchange produce, eggs and all that, or even labour, for the things they want. So if a peasant wants the services of an occultist the peasant will not think of giving money to the occultist because he doesn't have any, so instead he will provide the occultist with food, grain for example or fruit, and again, if he doesn't have any eggs or grain or fruit to spare, then he will do work for the occultist, mend his robes for example, carve a new bowl. If he had accommodation then the peasant will clean his accommodation. It may be a cave in the hillside and in that case the person who has used the occultist's service will clean the cave so many times, will sweep up the old grass and strew the floor with fresh grass. He will provide firewood and will do all necessary work.

It's still payment, though, isn't it? If he gives food, if he gives labour, it's still payment. But actually the warning against payment was a different matter altogether because the warning is against unscrupulous Westerners who advertise services they cannot really perform, and who are just out to make unreasonable charges. Some of the advertisements I have seen are truly too fantastic to be believed. It strikes me as most hilarious to think of a fellow packing his brief case and perhaps an overnight case and dashing off into the astral to read somebody's Akashic Record, always of course, for a high fee. Such things are impossible, they are quite impossible because there is a very strict occult law to the effect that no person can see the Akashic Record of another person who is alive. If you want to know what happened five hundred years ago, then that is a different matter, that is history and you can consult the Akashic Record in that case just as you can go to film libraries and pick out historical films. But just as many things are classified nowadays, you cannot report the speed of a certain plane or you cannot say how fast a certain shell goes, well, in much the same way you just cannot see or discuss the Akashic Record of a living person. After all, the Spirit World, you know, doesn't exist solely for some of these cranky advertisers; think of that when you read some of the advertisements, and have a laugh with me, will you?

CHAPTER SEVEN

Injure others and you injure
yourself.

THE day had been very pleasant, a clear blue sky and a warmer temperature than had been during the past few weeks. There were signs that the winter had ended and that spring was really thinking about peeping around the corner of the calendar and bringing warmth and sunshine and new life to those jaded and defeated by the frigid winters of Canada.

In the valleys snow was still thick and would remain so for perhaps a few weeks more, but in the higher ground exposed to the warming rays of the sun the snows were fast melting and trickling riverlets came rushing down to swell the Saint John River.

The day had seen many birds flying by, signs that spring was coming, birds returning to their old haunts; a whole covey of ducks went by, soon after a huge black-back seagull had come sweeping in from the sea to land on the roof and to peer about and utter raucous cries.

The evening had turned chilly. There was a hint of snow in the air. Suddenly, unexpectedly there came the drumming of hailstones beating rapidly upon the windows, bouncing off the balconies, and, for a few moments, carpeting the road with a white icy sheen.

The Old Man thought, 'Oh, poor Mr. Robichaud, he'll have to get busy again in the morning!' During the day Mr. Robichaud had been very busy sweeping aside puddles of melting snow, brushing away gravel thrown down by city trucks in an attempt to provide traction for motor traffic.

But now the hail had come driving fresh gravel into the front of the building and adding to the work of an already much overworked man.

The evening sped by and lights in the city went out one by one. In the Hospital the lights were ever on, always ready for emergencies, always ready by day and by night.

The Old Man turned his head and looked out of the window over the balcony; down in the Harbour there was still activity. The Russian ship loading grain for Russia was still a blaze of light. There was the clank of machinery and the hissing of high pressure steam.

Closer there was the terrible blare, and blare, and blare again as one of the Canadian National infernal diesel engines clattered along the rails over the level crossing, hooting and blaring as if the world had gone mad. 'I wonder that no one has told the engineer that there are signal lights on the crossing,' thought the Old Man, because it does seem insane how in Canada locomotives go along to the constant blare of sirens and the incessant clanging of bells. It's something like a gang of very small children playing with toys in the noisiest way possible. Canada, even more than the U.S.A., should be known as the Land of Noise and Bustle.

The Old Man lifted his gaze again beyond the level crossing and the endless procession of freight cars obstructing the road. In the Harbour tugs were coming to a Liberian ship which had just recently unloaded seven thousand tons of nickel ore. Earlier the ship had been arrested for non-payment of dues in the U.S.A. It had steamed away from a Pacific coast port apparently without the little formality of paying harbour dues, but the telephone was much faster than a ship and telephone messages had raced all across from the Pacific coast of the U.S.A. to the East coast of Canada, and earlier in the day Police officials had marched aboard the ship and served an arrest order to the Captain.

Frantic work had resulted in a bond being posted and now the ship was free to move, so tugs were coming to tow her out sternwards, tow her out backwards into the deep water channel and then, with her pointing in the right direction, off she would steam possibly for Australia.

The Pilot was already aboard, the Pilot boat was going out beyond the buoys waiting for the ship which would then slow and the Pilot boat would sidle along and take off the Pilot, and then the ship would be free to move away on her own.

The ship went out silently, no hooting, no clanking, no hissing of steam, the ship stole away as if she were ashamed of being arrested through the perfidy and bad faith of mankind, mankind as exemplified by those who should have paid the bills incurred for their service.

All over the city the sleeping people were leaving their physical bodies and going up into the astral worlds, their Silver Cords were stretched out like skins of silk, self-illuminated, shiny, twitching and jerking.

The Old Man smiled to himself because from one room came the soft snores of Buttercup. 'She'd never believe what a racket *she* is making!' thought the Old Man. Suddenly her astral form appeared through a wall and off she shot, straight up and then away in the direction of the U.S.A. With her astral out of her body the snores increased.

From another room Ra'ab was doing a bit of snoring too. She had gone off earlier to an astral Cat Land where she would be met by some truly beloved little people, Miss Ku'ei, Mrs. Fifi Greywhiskers, Miss Cindy, Long Tom, and Lord Furhead, and others. Ra'ab had the benefit that she was aware of when she was going to the Land of the Astral Cats, but probably Ra'ab was not aware of how stertorous her snores would be!

Little Girl Cat Cleopatra was sleeping away as well beside Ra'ab. She too was off to the Land of the Astral Cats, but Fat Cat Taddykins was on duty, she would be on duty until 4 o'clock in the morning, and Fat Cat Taddykins was resting on the shelf just above the radiator where she got all the warmth, all the beautifully heated rising air. One arm was dangling over, the other was supporting her chin. Her hind quarters were facing one way and her head quarters were facing another way, a position that only a cat could adopt.

Far out in the Bay of Fundy a fishing boat suddenly flashed its searchlight. It wavered around for a moment and then, as suddenly, was extinguished and there was no trace that a little fishing vessel was anywhere about. Yet all over the bay there were fishing vessels with their lines out and with their nets, hoping to get fish and that were not contaminated by the mercury in the water flowing from the U.S.A., from some big industrial plant in the U.S.A. which had discharged much poisonous effluvia into the streams passing by their boundaries. And yet there was a fresh source of poison because an oil tanker had broken up and sunk beneath the waves off the coast of Nova Scotia, and oil and poisoned birds and fish were being swept shorewards all the time. So the fishermen of New Brunswick were out about their business rather gloomily, knowing that their livelihood was at stake because of the criminal manner in which Man polluted the sources of Nature.

The sky had a few clouds scudding across, there seemed to be quite a wind coming up. The three flags away on the hill were flapping madly and the halyards were slapping against the masts as if in unison with the waving of the flags.

Over the hill beyond Mispec the full moon suddenly sailed with amazing rapidity straight up into a clear patch of sky, casting a pale brilliance over the whole scene, dimming the street lights, dimming the lights along the new bridge over the Saint John River, and as the moon rose the shaft of silver light sped rippling along the sea all the way from Mispec point to the Harbour, brilliant fingers touching a fishing vessel here, lighting a buoy there, silvering a strip of land and breaking up in ripples as it encountered the wake of a speeding tug.

The Old Man turned suddenly and a sharp, tearing, wrenching pain gripped him inside, a pain that left him gasping and almost retching with the sudden agony of it.

Pain, his constant companion for a long time past, pain which was becoming even more frequent and even more intense, pain which pointed with inexorable fingers at the calendar showing how the journey through life was progressing, showing how soon it must end.

On the shelf above the radiator Fat Cat Taddykins stood up, peered intently at the Old Man, muttered to herself, and went trotting into where Ra'ab was still asleep. Soon the Silver Cord attached between Ra'ab's astral and physical quivered and started to reel in, it reeled in with increasing rapidity until the astral body came as well. Seconds after Ra'ab came in to see what could be done for the Old Man, but what could be done? The Old Man had been in a state of permanent amazement since having 'medical treatment' in Canada. In his ignorance he had thought that the first duty of a doctor was the relief of suffering, that is what he had been taught. He had been taught that first of all you relieve the suffering, then you try to cure what caused it. But now – well, he saw the other side of the story, not as the doctor but as the patient.

The Old Man had had much pain and he and Ra'ab had asked the doctors for some pain relieving tablets, or anything. First they had been told, 'No, we do not want to give it yet, it might disguise the symptoms.' But in the meantime the Old Man still had his pain, still had his suffering, in the meantime the Old Man had been taken to hospital as a desperate emergency, and a compassionate nurse at the first hospital had done what the doctors did not seem able to do.

Then came the second emergency and another hospital, and the verdict that nothing could be done. So, knowing that nothing could be done to cure, the Old Man and Ra'ab and Buttercup just could not understand why it was that nothing could be done to relieve suffering, to ease the pain, to give rest for, to ask yet again, is not the doctor's first task the relief of suffering? And if he cannot cure the cause, then surely he can give relief while there is still life.

So Ra'ab looked around helplessly – what was there that she could do? There wasn't anything, she had no drugs, nothing. So once again she just had to sit and watch and give nothing else except sympathy and understanding.

Soon there came Cleopatra who did the feline equivalent of handsprings in the hope of distracting attention from pain, in the hope of providing some light relief, and Cleopatra and Taddykins both purred away to show how they understood how bad all this suffering was. Two little people who to the average man or woman in the street would appear to be just two very very beautiful little animals, but to those who know them these two little people are people apart, intelligent, highly civilized and entirely sympathetic and understanding.

And so the Old Man lying in his bed of pain still wondered why the local medical fraternity did not seem to have heard of pain relievers, or, if they had, why did they not use them, why did they not use such methods of giving relief to one who truly was in considerable distress?

Now the sky darkened, the moon was extinguished by black lowering clouds. A sudden haze came over the far sea and sped rapidly landwards, the first pattering drops of rain hit the window panes and a blast of air shook the building. Soon the storm burst in all its fury, the howling, shrieking wind and torrents of rain interspersed with hail. Down it came drowning out all memory of a pleasant day, hiding the Harbour under a veil of rain. Lights in the streets showed up as a ghostly greenish-blue as the sodium lamps vainly strove to penetrate the water fog and the beating rain.

The drumming of the rain was monotonous, the shrieking of the wind howling around the corners of the building, pushing against the windows, making the doors rattle, it reminded the Old Man of how things seemed to be inside him.

The night seemed endless, it seemed that every minute was an hour, and every hour was a day. Ra'ab, at the Old Man's request, went back to bed. Cleo stayed for a time, when she too went back to bed. Taddykins resumed her post on the shelf until 4 o'clock in the dark and gloomy morning. At 4 o'clock Miss Cleopatra came back into the room and jumped up by Taddy. Briefly they touched noses and Taddy jumped off leaving Miss Cleopatra to settle down into almost the same position that Taddy had adopted.

Outside the first traffic was beginning to move, early workers going to the docks. Down below a man started his car, perhaps he was going to the dry dock to see what was happening. A lonely tug hooted away as if lost in the rain and darkness. There was no sign of the lighthouse, the rain completely obscured its rays, but faintly could be heard the mournful lowing of the fog horn.

The hours dragged on. At last dim grey light appeared over the Mispec hills, a dim grey light which did little to dispel the gloom for it just showed a thoroughly unpleasant day, everything saturated with water. Water teeming from the rooftops, water streaming down the roadways, and suddenly squalls obliterating the sight of the bridge and the Harbour.

More hours passed on, and more people began to stir. Ra'ab came back, shortly after Buttercup came. Another day had started.

The Harbour looked almost empty. A Blue Star freighter was just turning into the stream ready to go out. She too was anxious to leave us. The Russian ship was still there with a faint plume of steam coming from its exhaust, and down on the D.O.T. wharf men were boarding one of the red-hulled ships that went out to take supplies to the lighthouse keepers and provide service to the light buoys and the sound buoys. In the middle of the Harbour a solitary tug was motionless, a figure at the stern seemed to be hauling in on a fishing line. Perhaps the tug men were trying to catch their breakfast!

The inevitable, incessant mail came pouring in. On this day with the Old Man feeling like something the cat brought in, seventy-eight letters came, nearly all of them from people who wanted something, nearly all of them without the elementary courtesy of a reply stamp.

One woman wrote so gushingly, 'Oh, Dr. Rampa, I have been told that you are going to die and I thought I must get your help before it was too late for me. Will you do this for me – you *must* do this for me before you die.'

People wrote in and wrote in, the Old Man did his best to answer reasonable questions. Buttercup worked hard and accurately typing the letters which the Old Man was now no longer able to do, but there was no let-up from people. So many of them, no sooner had they received a reply than they sent back a whole shoal of questions 'before it was too late'.

One 'lady' in Toronto sent seven letters all by one delivery. Apparently she wrote a letter of several pages and then when she'd got it all ready and posted she thought of other things she wanted to know, and so on, and so on, until seven letters had arrived.

The Old Man had many strange experiences with letters. One woman in Ontario wrote really inflammatory letters and managed to get hold of the Old Man's address. She got in touch with the Police and said it was desperately necessary to contact Dr. Rampa, it was a matter of life and death. And so our good-natured, well-intentioned local Police sent a police car to where the Old Man lived, to where the Old Man was ill, and the Policeman had a very stern order. 'You must phone this number immediately, it's a matter of life and death.' The same woman sent Special Delivery letters, telegrams – everything. And at last the Old Man couldn't stick it any longer, 'at last' was caused by a letter from the woman saying that unless the Old Man would be her 'friend' she would commit suicide and she enclosed three pages with just the same thing repeated, 'Die (name), Die (name), Die (name).' The Old Man could take no more so he got in touch with the Police in the district in which she lived, and the Police went along to see her about these letters of an 'amatory' nature. Now from that quarter at least, there has been peace, it is understood, though, that the poor unfortunate policeman who had to call upon her returned to the Station considerably shaken by the experience.

When the Old Man was at Habitat he was in bed one night quite seriously ill. At round about midnight there came a thunderous knocking at the door. Ra'ab hurried from her room and the Old Man managed to get out of bed and into the wheel chair, and to grasp something in case it was an unwanted intruder. But at the door were two French-Canadian policemen, and in decidedly shaky English they demanded to see Dr. Rampa. One of the policemen was from the fraud squad, the other was a police driver. They wanted to know all sorts of things, all manner of questions had to be answered, and at midnight. At last the Old Man wanted to know what it was all about, why were they asking so many questions, and the two policemen looked at each other and one walked to the telephone, then in a gabble of French-Canadian spoke to his Superintendent. After replacing the telephone their manner changed completely. He said that a man in the Middle West States of the U.S.A. had telephoned the Montreal Police Headquarters saying there was a desperate emergency and would the Police please contact Dr. Rampa, address unknown, and get him to call a certain number in that Middle West American State.

In relaying the message to the police on patrol the information was somewhat garbled, and because a fraud squad man took the message he thought he was coming to see the Old Man on a matter of fraud, and so he acted accordingly. However, at last matters were straightened out and the police left. Apologies were a bit late, well after midnight, and after rousing and distressing a very sick man.

The same thing happened when the Old Man lived in Saint John previously. The Police were phoned by some old biddy in Montreal. She said it was a matter of life and death, and so the police came up like eager beavers thinking they were going to save a life. The phone call was made and the stupid clot of a woman just wanted the Old Man to tell her husband that she shouldn't have any sex life with him! Incidentally, although considerable expense was involved, the woman and her husband have not made any attempt to repay that expense. That's what usually happens, some person just thinks that the Old Man is made of money and that he is just dying to rush to their aid and to pay them for that pleasure.

Quite recently a man wrote from Asia. He wrote to say that he wanted to do good for mankind, and he thought he would become a doctor, so he instructed the Old Man to send money immediately for this would-be doctor's first-class air fare to Canada. He told the Old Man that he (the Old Man) should have the honour of providing board and lodging and pay all expenses for this would-be doctor. He ended by writing, 'I can never repay you but at least you will know that I am doing good for others.'

Yet another case at Habitat was when a man came late at night complete with his luggage. He just came to the door and banged and banged until he got an answer. He came all the way from India, and he said, 'I have come to live with you as your son. I will cook for you.' And he tried to push his way in – complete with luggage.

The Old Man was thinking about these things, thinking about some of the humans who wrote in, thinking of the woman who wrote to say that her book was all ready, the book which the Old Man had dictated to her telepathically, and now she wanted a letter written by him saying that a Publisher was to take it and give the royalties to her.

A most entertaining book could be written about some of the remarkable letters which are sent, but really the Old Man in the short time remaining is far more interested in answering questions which it is hoped will help people. So many questions are quite sensible, questions such as this:

'Why is it that we never remember the tasks we are supposed to do when we are on this Earth? Why do we have to press forward blindly without knowing what we are doing? Can you tell me that?'

Well, yes, certainly, there is nothing very remarkable about it. If people knew beforehand what they had to do they would concentrate exclusively on that thing, and so gain a very one-sided knowledge or experience.

I am often told that I liken the Earth life to a school. But of course I do, it is a school, a school for humans. And so, going back to our school explanation, consider this; you study at school, but then you have to take an examination.

You have to take an examination. Yes, an examination to find out how much you know. You go to the examination room without knowing what the questions are going to be. If you knew the questions before you went to the examination room, then it would just not be an examination at all because you would just swot up a few sentences on a very few subjects, and obviously you would pass the examination with ease – but you wouldn't know anything.

At school one has to learn a broad field of knowledge, and to make sure that one does learn an adequately broad field of knowledge examinations are set for some future date. The students know that there is going to be an examination, but obviously they do not know the exact questions. Thus it is that they have to study the whole field which will be covered by the examinations, and not specialize in just one or two items.

Supposing a surgeon, or rather, surgeon-to-be, was taking his examinations and he had been slack throughout his studies, supposing that someone had told him the precise nature of the questions. If the surgeon-to-be was unscrupulous and unprincipled he would concentrate only on the answers to those questions and, of course, would pass 'cum laude'.

But you might be his first patient. Supposing you went for a kidney operation and all he could do was remove an appendix – would you feel happy?

Would you feel happy in dealing or flying with an air pilot who, by knowing the answers to the exact examination questions and knowing little else, had managed to get a job? Of course you wouldn't.

You are kept from knowing what your task is in this life so that you do your best (or at least it is hoped that you will!) in the whole field of life. You might have a task that you have to be kind to cats; well, if you knew what you had to do you might be very kind to cats, sickeningly so, in fact, but you might be so wrapped up in the cat theme that you would perhaps unwittingly cause anguish to dogs or horses by completely and utterly neglecting them. No, Mrs. Questioner, it is providential that humans do not know their task on Earth. If they did it would make them unbalanced and one-sided.

But do not get the idea that everyone who writes is a dumkopf or clutterhead, such would be absolutely incorrect. I have become acquainted with some extraordinarily nice people. Valeria Sorock, for one. She was the first to greet me when we arrived from Ireland, since that we have been firm friends and Valeria Sorock has an absolutely wonderful virtue; she is completely and utterly reliable. I am not at all mobile and if there is anything in particular that I need, of course always something which is extremely difficult to obtain, then Valeria Sorock is the one to locate it. We live quite a long way apart physically, but we are very close spiritually.

Let me salute Valeria Sorock here for her unfailing constancy, for her loyalty, and for the immense effort she puts in to do any kindness. She is not a wealthy woman by any means at all, in fact she has to work hard and travel many miles to earn what is truly a mere pittance, yet Valeria Sorock can always afford the time to do anything and to help. So – Valeria – my thanks to you and my undying friendship to you in return for the friendship you have always given me.

There are quite a number of people who are definitely above average, very definitely above average, and it's a sad thought that these people most times are not at all well endowed with this world's goods. Most times these people are so decent and so modest that they definitely underrate their own abilities. I am thinking now of two very brilliant people, Mr. and Mrs. Czermak. They are having a difficult time because, in my opinion, they do not 'sell themselves'.

Mr. Czermak is a man whom anyone could be proud to know, a man of the better type, a man with a first-class brain, and who excels at something which always defeats me — *figures*! Figures that go 1 – 2 – 3, etc., not the type that one looks at although I have no doubt that Mr. Czermak could possibly beat me at looking at those.

Then there is Mrs. Czermak, a truly very, very gifted person indeed. She has most extraordinary artistic ability, ceramics, photography, anything in the artistic line seems to be child's play to her. She puts the brakes on her own progress, though, by tending to be too much of a perfectionist. One cannot have perfection in this world, and if one strives too much for utter perfection then one wastes too much time on the unattainable.

Soon we shall be dealing with two questions, one from Mr. Czermak and one from Mrs. Czermak.

Yes, people write to me with all sorts of strange problems, and the longest letter I have received from any one person was written on a piece of paper 9 inches wide by 13 feet 9 inches long. It was all one continuous sheet of paper and the whole thing was closely typed. So, as I say, that is the longest letter I have had. What would *you* do with it? So did I!

Then, of course, there's John Henderson. I became acquainted with him following a letter or two that he wrote to me. John Henderson is a very nice fellow, very capable, and he's 'going places'. It is my hope that later he will be able to unfold his spiritual wings and write a book or two, start a Spiritual Retreat, and do whatever people on the Other Side suggest that he should do.

Yes, I make some very nice acquaintanceships. Some people who write in haven't the vaguest interest in metaphysics, but what does it matter, what does it matter if one is interested in metaphysics or not? In fact, it might be a good idea now to answer a question from Mr. Hanns Czermak. He says, 'Yes, I do have a question, Dr. Rampa. What is the most important thing a person should or can do to develop any latent occult abilities he or she might possess? I am asking this because I seem to have trouble getting started with the things you describe so clearly in your books. Obviously I am doing something wrong and I am wondering whether there isn't a way of preparing one's mind and body.'

Actually, it doesn't really matter if you do astral travel or not, consciously, that is, because everyone does astral travel in the time of sleep. But if you find difficulty in doing something, then are you sure, really sure, that you want to do it? Are you sure that there is not some bar imposed, let us say, by difficulties in a past life?

Supposing a person – oh, not you, of course! – had been a witch in a past life. Supposing you had been burned at the stake or bumped off in some equally interesting way, then if you came back to this life with more or less of an interest in occultism you might have some ingrained fear that if you started again you would end up at the stake or at the end of a rope, and so your sub-conscious would clap the brakes on and you would make no progress.

The only way one can proceed if one finds real difficulty in settling down to occult work is:

Meditate on the problem. Do you really, sincerely desire to astral travel or to do clairvoyance or read the cards or do anything in that field?

If you do, if you can say 'Yes', then ask yourself why you want to do it. You must clear up all these problems first.

The next thing to ask yourself is, do you fear that you will be out of the body and will not be able to get back, are you afraid that some strange entities will attack you if you get out of the body? If so, remember that no harm whatsoever, no harm of any sort can happen to you if you are not afraid.

If you are sure that you really want to do occult work, then the best thing is to devote a certain time each day, even half an hour of an evening, to thinking about it. And the best way is to imagine as strongly as possible that you are doing what you want to do, because when you can get over to your sub-conscious that you want to get out into the astral he will, metaphorically, unlock the gate and set you free. Think of the sub-conscious as a sort of idiot, a high-grade idiot, if you like, who obeys orders quite literally so that if at some time in the past you have said, 'Gee! For Pete's sake don't let me get out of the body!' then the subconscious will obey that injunction until you can overpower its one-track mind and replace the obsolete order by another.

But remember that if you think you are not making progress, you definitely are so long as you are aware of things. And my strong advice to you is that if you are experiencing obstacles or difficulties, then just do not bother, wait until things settle themselves.

When I was studying morse many years ago I was warned about 'the hump'. Well, this mysterious 'hump' bothered me until I reached a speed of twenty-three words a minute, and no matter how much I tried, no matter how many hours of practice I put in, I could not get over that 'hump'. It proved to be a mountain in the way of my progress towards a faster morse sending and receiving speed.

One day I uttered some really naughty words with fervour. I said, in effect, 'Oh well, if I can't go any faster I just can't.' Later in the day I sat down at the old morse key again and found that I could go much faster, in fact I could do nearly thirty words a minute. I had got over the 'hump'. I had been trying too hard, and I think probably you are trying too hard, Mr. Czermak, and you, and you, and you also are trying too hard. If you are meeting obstacles don't go on like a bulldozer, take it easy, think about things, and you will find that the path of least resistance has enabled you to get over the hump, and you will be surprised at the result.

Well, I think that in the interests of domestic harmony I should reply to a question from Mrs. Czermak in this same chapter as that in which I replied to a question from her husband, otherwise I could be accused of separating husband and wife, or something like that.

Here is what Mrs. Czermak writes. 'A question; well, by the time it's too late to submit them I know I will be full of them. Right now there is only one problem that is still very much with me, and maybe other people might profit too if you would be kind enough to say a few words on the topic. It's time, or rather, shortage of time. There are only so many hours in the day and they just are not sufficient to do all the things I want to do. I surely don't shirk work but what is most frustrating is that not only is there not enough time for all the more or less mundane things that one wants to do, but there never seems enough left for the spiritual things one wants to learn. If it's meditation I don't seem to have enough energy to get up extra early either on Saturday or Sunday, instead of sleeping an hour later, and if it's astral travel I seem to fall asleep as soon as I hit the pillow.'

Business firms, factories, and very large offices have the same trouble, that is why they often call in experts who call themselves 'Time and Motion' people. Everyone has three or four times as much time as they think they have, but usually people waste time in much the same way as people waste water and so now there is a shortage of water throughout the world, drinking water, that is.

Time and motion experts study how people do things. Just as an example, if you go to the kitchen how many things do you bring back with you at one time? Do you bring back one or two things when you know perfectly well that right after you will have to go back for two or three things more? If people will only make an intelligent appraisal of things they have to do, then they will have adequate time in which to do it.

The best way to proceed is to write down on a sheet of paper all the things you want to do on any given day. Toss out the things which are not really necessary, and plan the remaining things so that you go the shortest way about them and do not have to make two or three journeys when one will suffice. Some people have shopping to do, so they dash around to the corner store and get one thing, then they return to the kitchen and find they are short of salt or sugar or something else, so back they go again. They are running about all the time.

Others, perhaps, have letters to mail, and they make a special journey to mail those letters whereas, if they only waited a little longer, they could mail the letters when they went shopping.

One can divide up the day just the same as at school lessons were divided up – so long for Geography, so long for History, so long for Arithmetic, so long for recreation and so long for meals. If people only set about their tasks in a sensible manner they would have ample time in which to do things.

In Mrs. Czermak's case, she has a highly intelligent husband who would gladly assist her in planning her days. A task which he is well fitted to undertake very successfully.

So the answer is, if people would plan their days properly and stick to the plan, there would be adequate time for everything. This is the Voice of Experience because I practise what I preach – successfully!

CHAPTER EIGHT

If you don't scale the mountain
you can't view the plain.

THE Old Man resting in his bed was looking out across the city, looking out at some new building being built, and at a very large hotel, the leading hotel in the whole city.

Miss Cleo and Miss Taddy were busy sleeping. They had had a disturbed night because the Old Man had been very unwell and, of course, it definitely takes two Siamese cats to manage things when the Old Man is particularly unwell. So they were catching up on their sleep, moving about in their sleep as all the best people do, twitching a bit, but happy to be close to each other. The Old Man thought of them with absolute love, thought of them as he would have thought of his own children, for these were very high entities in animal form, little people who had come to do a job and who were doing that job magnificently.

In their four short years of life they had had quite a bit of moving about, quite a bit of travel, and quite a bit of hardship, hardship largely brought on by the incessant press persecution. The Old Man lay there in the gloaming thinking about it all, thinking of conditions at Montreal, and how they had left before their tenancy had ended.

They had made arrangements for accommodation in the city of Saint John but when it was too late to change anything the person still in the apartment found he was unable to leave, so The Family had no alternative to staying expensively in an hotel; the Admiral Beatty Hotel was truly as much of a home from home as any hotel could be. It was and is a happy hotel where everyone is satisfied with the General

Manager, a man with years and years of experience, a man who knows all the problems and, better still, knows the answers to them.

In the hotel one of the bell boys, Brian, was always most helpful and most courteous, and being a cat lover he really fell for Miss Cleo and Miss Taddy, and that pair, being flirts like most girls, really played him up, purred for him, rubbed against him and, like most girls, made him think that he was *the* only one.

They made a friend at the hotel of yet another person, Mrs. Catherine Mayes. The Old Man had a lot of difficulty with diet, and the menu of a hotel is not designed for those who are sick and limited to certain foods. Mrs. Catherine Mayes went out of her way at all times to make sure that everything was as good as could be. Now that The Family were in an apartment they still welcomed Mrs. Mayes as a visitor.

But the lights in the Harbour were becoming more and more numerous. Ships were coming in ready to discharge their cargoes at the next working day. Two Russian ships, another one from Liberia, one from India, and one from Cyprus, all moored up along the wharves, all laden down, well down to their plimsoll line, and a gently swaying at the changing of the tide.

The Pilot Boat was just coming away from a newcomer, its red signal lamp blinking and bobbing. Soon it turned right and went into its slipway so the Pilots could wait for the next ship.

Down at the level crossing the infernal trains hooted and blared away, making such a commotion as would get any other person clapped straight into prison for disturbing the peace, yet these unmentionable railway workers seemed to think it was their prerogative and sacred duty to wreck the hearing of a whole city. The Old Man wondered why the City Council didn't get off their behinds and pass that long-protected law prohibiting the blaring of sirens from trains passing through the city.

But the Old Man thought, it's useless to do idle gazing when a book has to be written, so he thought he would have to do what the City Council should do, he thought he would have to 'get off his behind' and get to work.

Going through all the questions, one of the most amazing things is the number of people who write 'tell us about life after death and about dying'. I am almost ashamed to return to that subject which I have dealt with so many times, I am almost ashamed to tell Ra'ab that I am writing about death again, and I am almost frightened to think of Buttercup's stony glare when she tells me that I am repeating myself. But then, Miss Newman, or perhaps it is Mrs. Newman, asks about life after death, and another letter here wants 'a complete but understandable knowledge of the so-called after-death state'. Riffling through these questions I find more and more people asking about life after death. Well, I seem to be ruled out, it seems that I shall have to write about life after death, and if you don't want to read it, go through these pages with your eyes shut until you come to a part you like.

Let us consider what happens at the onset of death. Usually a person is ill and as a result of that illness some part of the body, essential to the continuance of life on Earth, is losing its ability to function properly. It may be the heart, let us pretend that it is a heart case which we are discussing. So, in our heart case we can say that the heart muscle has turned into a fibroid mass, it can no longer pump blood in adequate quantities through the brain, and so the faculties become dull. As the faculties become dull the will to live diminishes and there is less stimulation for the heart to continue its laboured pumping.

There comes a time when the heart can no longer continue. Before that stage is reached the person is in a state where he does not have the energy to feel pain, he is half in this world and half in the next, he is in the state of a baby who is half out of the world which is his mother and half in the world which we call Earth. On the Other Side of death helpers are ready. As soon as the heart ceases there is a jerk; no, no, that is not a jerk of pain, there is no death agony, that is quite stupid fiction. The so-called 'death agony' is merely a reflex action of nerves and muscles which, freed from the control of the 'driver' of the body just twist and twitch and jerk — well, as the name implies — uncontrollably. Many people think that it is agony but of course it is not because the occupant of the body has left, and should there be grimaces of the face, that is merely the twitching of the muscles.

The body, bereft of its occupant, may twitch or utter gasps for a short time. There may be the rumbling of organs within the body, but all that is just like an old suit of clothes settling down after they have just been thrown on a chair or on a bed, there's nothing to it, the body is now just garbage ready to be buried or burnt, it doesn't matter which really.

The newest occupant or inhabitant of the astral world, the former driver of the body, will be met by helpers ready to do anything they can to assist in the process of acclimatization. It sometimes happens unfortunately that a truly ignorant person will not believe in life after death, so what then?

If a person definitely refuses to believe in the life after death he or she is in a state of complete hypnosis, auto-hypnosis, and even on Earth there are many cases of people being blind just because they think they are, there are many cases of people who are deaf only because they have wished themselves deaf perhaps to escape the noise of a nagging wife, and such cases are attested by the medical profession.

If a person will not believe in anything after death, then that person is enveloped in a thick, black, sticky fog, and helpers cannot help him, they can't reach him because he won't let them, he repulses everything they want to do for him because he is so convinced that there is no such thing as an after life that he believes he is having unpleasant nightmares.

In the course of time the person begins to realize that

there must be something in this life after death business after all; why does he hear voices, why does he sense people near him, why does he hear perhaps music? With dawning awareness that there might just possibly be something after death, the thick black fog lightens and becomes grey, light can filter in, he can see dim figures moving about, and he can hear more clearly. So, gradually, as his prejudices and inhibitions break down, he becomes more and more aware that something is happening around him. People constantly try to help him, they try to tell him that they want to help, they invite him to accept that help, and as soon as he does feel that he will accept help, then the fog disperses and he can see all the glory of the astral world, colours such as Earth lacks, brightness and lightness, and very very pleasant surroundings.

Our poor friend, who is only just beginning to realize that there is life after death, is taken to what we might call a hospital, or rest home, or recuperation centre. There by various rays his mental inhibitions are further dispersed, his spirit body is strengthened and made healthy, and it is also nourished.

Things are explained to him, he is in much the same position as a new-born baby except that he can understand all that is said to him and he can reply whereas a baby has to learn even to speak. So the person hears an explanation of what life on the Other Side is like. If he wants to argue about it he just cannot, people will not argue with him, he is just left to think about what he has been told, and when he can freely accept that which he has been told, the explanation continues. He is never persuaded of anything, he is never forced to do anything, he has a right of choice. If he doesn't want to believe then he has to stay in a somewhat static condition until he will believe.

Many there are who pass beyond the Earth to the next life with the firm, absolutely unbreakable conviction that their own particular religion is the only one which can exist. These poor wretches are in much the same position because the helpers on the Other Side know quite well that they cannot help the newcomer if their mere appearance shatters a lifelong belief, so, let us suppose a person is a very strong Catholic believing in angels and devils and all the rest of that pantomime. Then, when they get to the Other Side they do indeed see the Pearly Gates, they see an old fellow with a beard and a whacking great ledger in which they think all the sins are being recorded.

Everything is done to put on the sort of show that the good, ignorant Catholic wants to see. He sees angels with flapping wings, he sees people sitting on clouds playing harps, and for a time he is quite satisfied thinking he has reached Heaven. But gradually it dawns on him that all this doesn't ring true, the people do not fly in the right rhythm for beating wings, etc., etc. Gradually it dawns on the newcomer that all this is a stage show and he begins to wonder what is behind it all, what is behind the drapes and the set piece, what are things really like, and just as soon as he begins to think that way he begins to see 'cracks' in the facade of the Heavenly Crowd. Soon there comes a time when he cannot stick the pantomime any longer and he cries out for enlightenment. Quickly the angels with their flapping wings fade away, quickly the harpists sitting in their nightshirts on a cloud beat it, quickly highly trained, highly experienced helpers show the newly awakened newcomer the reality instead of the illusion, and the reality is far greater than the illusion ever could be. It is a sad fact that so many people see a few pictures in the Bible and they 'take them for gospel'. Well, book illustrators are employed to illustrate the Bible as well, remember.

No matter what religion it is, if there are adherents who believe unswervingly in the legends and, let us say, fantasies, of that religion, then that is what they see when they leave the Earth and enter the astral plane.

When the newcomer can realize the nature of the world he is in, then he can proceed further. He goes to the Hall of Memories and there, alone, he enters a room and he sees the whole of his life, everything he has done, everything he has tried to do, and everything he wanted to do. He sees everything that happened to him, and everything that he thought while upon the Earth, and he, and he alone, can make a judgment of whether his life was a success or a failure.

He, and he alone, can decide whether he will 'go back to college' and start the Course all over again in the hope of passing successfully next time.

There is no mother or father or best friend to stand by and take the blame for anything that he has done wrongly, he is there alone, entirely alone, more alone than he has been since he stood in that place before, last time. And he judges himself.

No devils, no Satan waiting with twitching tail and fiery breath, nobody is going to jab pitchforks into him, and as for all the flames, well, they don't even use such things for central heating!

Most people emerge from the Hall of Memories considerably shaken and remarkably glad of the help and sympathy which their helpers, waiting outside, offer.

There comes a period of adjustment, a period when the newcomer can think over all that he has seen, think over all the mistakes he has made, think over what he is going to do about it. It's not a matter to be decided in a few minutes, all manner of things have to be considered. Is it worth going back and starting all over again, or would it be better to stay a few hundred years in the astral waiting perhaps for more suitable conditions to come along? But then, thinks the newcomer, he doesn't know about all the suitable conditions or when they are likely to come along. So he is invited to go to helpers who will discuss everything with him, and who will advise him without putting any pressure whatever on him. At all times he has complete freedom of choice, freedom of decision, no one is going to force him to do anything. If he wants to go back and do a bit of hell-raking on Earth, that is his choice, and his choice only.

Many newcomers are not aware that they can pick up all

the sustenance, all the nourishment they need from the air, from the vibrations around them. They think of their earthly life, they think of all the choice foods they would have liked to have had but perhaps couldn't afford, so, if they want it they can have it. No matter what type of food, it is there for the asking. If they want fat cigars or thin cigarettes or stinking pipes, yes, they can have those as well. Clothes – you'll never see such a medley of clothes and costumes as you will on the astral plane! Anyone can wear any style of clothes he desires and it's not considered at all wrong, no one cares, it's the other person's affair. So if a fellow wants to get himself done up as a hippy with a load of' pot on each hand, he can do so, the pot there won't hurt him, it only hurts when he's on the earth because astral pot is entirely harmless; Earth pot is horribly dangerous.

But the newcomer soon tires of doing nothing, he soon tires of just kicking his heels and watching the astral world go by. Even if he was a lazy slob on Earth, one who just liked to hang around street corners and utter wolf whistles, well even that sort of fellow soon tires of doing nothing in the atmosphere of the astral plane. He asks for work, and he gets it. What sort of work? There are all manner of things to be done. It's impossible to say what sort of work he does just as it's impossible to say what sort of work a person would get here on Earth if they went to Timbuctoo or Alsace Lorraine suddenly. They do work within their capabilities, necessary work, and in doing the work they find considerable satisfaction and stability.

But all the time they have the nagging thought, the nagging wonder of what to do. Should they stay in the astral a bit longer? What would other people do? They ask again and again, and they are told again and again, always the same thing they are told, and never is there any attempt to persuade them to do anything, the choice is entirely theirs.

At last they decide they can't hang around any longer, they decide they cannot be a drop-out from the school of

Earth, they must go back, do their lessons properly and pass the examinations.

They make their decision known and then they are taken to a special group of people who have vast experience and some very, very remarkable instruments. It is determined what the person has to learn, it is determined how best he may learn it – go to a poor family, will that help? Or should he go to a rich family? Should he be a white man or a coloured man, or should he be a woman, coloured or white? It depends on the sort of mess he made of his last life, it depends on how hard he is prepared to work in the coming life, it depends on what he has to learn. Anyhow, the advisers are well qualified to help him, they can suggest – and they suggest only – the type of parents, the type of country, and the conditions. Then when he has agreed to the conditions certain instruments are brought into play and the necessary parents-to-be are located. Alternative parents are located as well, and these parents are observed for a short time. Then, if everything proves satisfactory, the person who is ready to reincarnate goes to a special home in the astral world. There he goes to bed, and when he wakes up he is in the process of being born into the Earth. No wonder he makes such a commotion and lets out wails of despair!

Many people, entities, decide they do not want to return to Earth just yet, and so they stay in the astral worlds where they have much work to do. But before discussing them let us deal with a special class of people who have no choice; suicides.

If a person has wilfully ended his or her life on Earth before the allotted number of years, then that person has to return to Earth as fast as possible in order to serve out the unexpired time, just as if they were a convict who had escaped and had been recaptured, and had had a bit tacked on as an extra punishment.

A suicide gets into the astral world. He is met, received, just as if he were an ordinary legitimate person coming back, no recriminations, nothing of that type at all. He is treated precisely the same as other entrants. He is allowed a reason-able time in which to recover from the shock of leaving the physical body probably violently, and entering the astral.

When he has recovered sufficiently he has to go to the Hall of Memories, and there he sees all that has ever happened to him, he sees the flaws which really made him commit suicide. And so he is left with the awful feeling, the awful knowledge would be a better term, that he has to get back to Earth and live out the unexpired term.

Possibly the suicide is a person of poor spiritual calibre, possibly he lacks the intestinal fortitude to go back on Earth, and he thinks he is just jolly well going to stay in the astral and nobody can do anything about it. Well, he is wrong there because it is a law that a suicide has to return to Earth, and if he will not return of his own free will, then he is compelled to go.

If he is willing to return, then, at a meeting with special counsellors, he is advised of how many days or years there are remaining to him on his Earth 'sentence'. He has to live out all that time on Earth, he also has to live out all the time that has elapsed since he committed suicide and before returning to Earth again. So, perhaps it took a year to straighten him out and get him to decide that he had to go back to Earth, thus he gets a year added to his life on Earth.

Conditions are found on Earth so that he can return and encounter substantially the same type of conditions which caused him to take his life before, and then at the appointed time he is put to sleep and awakens to the act of being born.

If he proves recalcitrant and just will make no move to go back to Earth, then the counsellors decide for him on conditions which would meet his case. If he will not go freely then the conditions are a bit tougher than if he did go freely. Then, again at the appointed time, he is put to sleep without him having any choice whatever in the matter, he is put to sleep and when he wakes up he is back on Earth.

It is often the case that a baby who is born and dies perhaps a month or two after is the reincarnation of a person who committed suicide rather than perhaps face two or three months of agony when they were dying from incurable, inoperable cancer. The sufferer may have taken his own life two or three, or perhaps six months or a year before he would naturally have died. But he still has to come back and serve out all the time which he tried to short-circuit.

It is sometimes thought that pain is a useless thing, suffering is a useless thing. It is sometimes thought that it is good to kill off a human who is incurable, but do these people who advocate such a course really know what the sufferer is trying to learn? His very suffering, the very nature of his illness may be something about which he desired to learn.

People often write to me and say, 'Oh, Dr. Rampa, with all your knowledge how is it that you have to suffer so? Why don't you cure yourself and live for ever?' But, of course, that's nonsense. Who wants to live for ever? And people who write in with statements like that, how do they know what I am trying to do? They don't, and that's all there is to it. If a person is investigating a certain subject then often that person has to undergo a considerable amount of hardship in order to do the work properly. These people who wander off and bring aid and sustenance to lepers, for instance, well, they don't know how the leper feels or how the leper thinks. They might be helping the leper's physical being, but they still are not lepers. Its the same with T.B., or cancer, or even an ingrowing toenail. Until one actually has the complaint or the condition then one quite definitely is not qualified to make any discussion on the complaint or condition. It always amuses me that Roman Catholic priests who are not married and who, presumably never have children, never become a father, that is, except in the spiritual sense, dare to advise women about having children and all that. Of course many of these Catholic priests go away for vacations and they get to know quite a lot about women. We saw that in Montreal!

It is definitely wrong, then, to commit suicide. You are just postponing the day when you can be free of Earth legitimately, you've got to come back like an escaped convict who has been recaptured, and you are hurting no one but yourself, and it's yourself you think about, isn't it? That's one of the things that has to be overcome, too.

The ordinary average person who is not too good and not too bad stays in the astral world for a varying period of time. It is not true that everyone stays there for six hundred, or a thousand, or two thousand years; it depends entirely on the conditions which prevail in the case of each and every individual. There is an average time, but then there is an average man-in-the-street and an average woman-in-the-street, and the average time is just – well, just a figure.

There are many tasks to do in the astral world. Some people help those who are coming to join the astral world, some people act as guides to them, and this 'guide' has nothing to do with spiritualist seances or old ladies who think they have a Red Indian guide or a Chinese Mandarin guide or a Tibetan Lama guide. What these old ladies usually have is an overdose of imagination. Actually, if everything was counted up and if everyone who claimed to have an Indian guide or a Tibetan guide was listed, there just wouldn't be enough Indians or enough Tibetans to go round, and in any case these people on the Other Side have their own jobs to do, and those jobs do not include stirring teacups so some old biddy can give a reading, it doesn't include speaking through a tin trumpet or moving a bit of cheesecloth. All that stuff, which of course is utterly useless, comes from a bit of nervous energy on the part of some usually hysterical operator. People on the Other Side have too much to do looking after their own affairs to come to Earth and poke about in dark rooms breathing down the necks of people who are there for a delicious thrill. The only ones who do go to these seances from the Other Side are the Nature Spirits of a lower type called Elementals. They are there just for some fun, to see what a lot of saps these humans are to believe anything and everything that is told to them. Don't you, my dear friends Reader, go in for this guff, because guff it is.

The same goes for this Ouija Board stuff. People will get a Ouija Board and play about with it, and some Elemental who is always dashing about like a mischievous monkey, will see what is being done, and he will definitely influence the reading. Now you might think there is no harm in that, but there is no good in it either, and definitely there is great harm in these Ouija Board readings if an Elemental causes the message to be given to sound highly plausible but which is just something extracted from the victim's own sub-conscious. A person's whole life can be affected for the worse by believing in this Ouija Board messages.

Another great source of misinformation is when the Ouija Board is moved in accordance with the collective thought of the people who are gathered around. Often it will be impelled by wishful thinking and, again, will give a message which can be positively harmful by being misleading. The safest thing is — have nothing whatever to do with Ouija Boards and nothing whatefer to do with seances. Remember, you came to this Earth deliberately not knowing the exact purpose of your visit, and if you try to find out too much without very, very exceptional cause, then you are like the student going to the examination room who manages to steal a copy of the examination papers first. That is just plain cheating, and it doesn't help at all.

One job which has to be done in the astral world is to receive those who come during the hours of sleep. People are arriving at all times because when it is daylight in one part of the world it is night in another part, so there are a constant stream of people going to the astral world during their sleep period, and they are like children returning from school. Just as children like to be greeted by their parents or friends, so do these night travellers.

Their traffic has to be directed, they have to be put in touch with those whom they desire to meet, and many of them desire information and counselling during what, upon Earth, is night. They want to know how they are doing and what they should do on the morrow. This does occupy a lot of time for a lot of people.

Then there are other entities in the astral world who are not reincarnating to Earth again, they are going on – going up, going up to an even higher plane of existence. At the right time they will 'die' very peacefully, very painlessly to the astral world. They will, in fact, just vanish to the astral world and will appear in a higher plane.

There are more and more people coming to the Earth, more and more people being born to the Earth, and many inquirers wonder why that should be so. The answer is Earth is just one speck of dust amid billions of specks of dust, and when people ask me why the population of the Earth is increasing I tell them the truth, which is that people are coming to Earth from other more nebulous planes of existence. Perhaps a person comes from a two dimensional world and comes to Earth as his first experience in a three dimensional world, so he starts his round of existence to the three dimensional world which we call Earth. And all the time there are more and more people coming as Earth becomes more and more of a qualified school of hardship. That is the purpose of Earth, you know, to teach one hardship and how to endure it and how to overcome it. People do not come to Earth to have a very enjoyable time, they come to learn so that all the information they learn can be passed on to the Overself.

After this world there is the astral plane, and from the astral plane, in the fullness of time, one is born upwards to different planes of existence until at last the fully evolved entity merges with the Overself. That is how the Overself grows.

If, having grown quite a lot, the Overself decides that there is much more to learn, then fresh 'puppets' are put down on some world and the whole process of cycles of life is started all over again, and each time when the puppets have completed their cycles they return purified to the Overself, which, again, grows through it.

When a person is living in the astral, that is, when a

133

person has 'died' to Earth, then that particular entity enters into the full life of the astral world and is not just a visitor as are those who return to the astral world during that time when their body is asleep on the Earth, and, being full-time members of the astral world, they behave as ordinary people would on the Earth. That is, at the end of an astral day they sleep. The astral body which, of course, is quite solid to people in the astral world, goes to sleep, and, again, the psyche leaves the astral body at the end of its Silver Cord and goes into a yet higher plane. There it learns things which will be of use on what we might term the lower astral when the spirit returns to the astral body. Do not think that the astral world is the highest world, do not think that it is Heaven; it is not. There are many, many different cycles or planes of existence.

While in that world which we call 'the astral world' we can have a family. We live in much the same way as people live down here except that there are not quarrels because in the astral you just cannot meet people with whom you are incompatible. So that if you get married in the astral, then you cannot have a nagging partner. This is not generally understood by people on Earth; while in the astral world you cannot meet those who were your enemies on Earth, and your family – well, your astral family are as solid to you as were people on the Earth to you.

Humans are not alone in the astral world, animals go there too. Never, never make the most tragic mistake of thinking that humans are the highest form of existence; they are not. Humans are just another form of existence. Humans think in one way, animals think in another way, but there are entities who, compared to humans, are as much above the humans as the humans are above the earthworms, and even these People know that they are not the ultimate form of evolution. So forget all about being a superior creature and concentrate on doing the best job you can.

Animals go to the astral plane, animals go higher as they merit it just as humans do. One of the big difficulties with the Christian religion is that they think humanity is the highest form of evolution possible, they think that all creatures were made for the satisfaction of Man, and that has led to some terrible conditions. The animal world and the animal Manus have been incredibly tolerant knowing that humans have been misinstructed by their religious leaders, by their priests who really rearranged Christianity to give themselves adequate power.

Accept it as fact, then, that in the astral worlds you will not find cowering dogs or scared cats. You will instead find a partner who is in every way the equal of a human and who can communicate with a human with utter ease by telepathy.

Many people have asked about bodies, will a body appear to be just a bunch of gas, or what? And the answer is, no, a body will appear as solid to you in the astral as is that lump of me at which you now push about on two bony stems, and if two people should collide in the astral, well, they get a bump just the same as when two people collide on the Earth plane.

There is great love in the astral world, physical love as well as spiritual love but, of course, on a scale which the mind limited to Earth thoughts cannot comprehend while in the Earth body. There is no such thing as 'frustration' in the astral world because love is completely satisfactory at all times and for both partners.

Some people have written in asking for a description of God. God is not just the Head of a big Corporation, you know, He's not just an old fellow who wears a long beard and carries a lantern on the end of a staff. God is a great Force which can be comprehended and understood when one is out of the Earth body and in the astral world. At present upon the Earth one is in a three dimensional world and most people could not understand, let us say, the description of a nine dimensional object.

Each world has a Manu in charge of the world. You can say that the Manu is like one of the Gods on Olympus so thoroughly described in Greek legends. Or if you wanted to be more up to date you can say that the Manu is like the General Manager of the branch of a big firm. Under the General Manager of that branch – because this world is only a branch, after all – we have departmental managers who, in our terms, would be called the Manus of different continents and of different countries. These under managers are responsible for running, let us say, the U.S.A. or Germany or Argentina, and so on, and just as human managers have different temperaments so do the Manus, and so the country concerned gets a different national characteristic. The Germans, for example, are quite different from the Italians, and the Italians are quite different from the Chinese. That is because the 'Manager' of that department happens to be different.

The Manus, no matter how glorious they seem to be, are just puppets of the Great Entity or Overself which makes up 'God'. That Great Overself uses Manus as puppets in much the same way as the human Overself may use a whole bunch of humans in order to gain experience.

Another question which is so frequently asked is, 'The astral body apparently has some sort of substance to it. If it has molecules, no matter how thinly dispersed, these could be subject to destruction or injury through heat, cold, or collision. If this were so some discomfort and pain in almost a physical sense could exist. How would the astral fare in the vicinity of a physical star?' Well, when one talks of molecules one is talking of substances which are in the Earth plane. A molecule is a physical thing, a piece of matter, but when we are talking about the astral plane we are completely away from the low grade vibration which comprises everything upon this Earth. A physical body on the Earth can receive injury from another physical body, but a physical body in the astral cannot in any way be damaged by the physical body of the Earth, the two things are completely and utterly different. One can say, just purely as an example and not a very good example at that, one can say that a rock

and a light do not interact upon each other. If we throw a
rock up into the sky it doesn't hurt the sun. So in the same
way anything that happens on the Earth does not hurt any
astral body, but what does hurt people in the astral is the
crass stupidity displayed by humans on the Earth in trying
to bump each other off, liquidate each other in various pain-
ful ways, and generally behave like a lot of completely
insane people instead of entities who are upon Earth to
learn something. The way people of Earth as going on at the
present time is much the same as the way the students who
wreck million dollar computers are going on. It's time
humans grew up, and it's time students learned that they go
to a school or college to learn from people who know more
than they do.

CHAPTER NINE

Remember, the turtle progresses
only when he sticks out his neck.

GLORY be! I thought I had put behind me all discussion of astrals, deaths, and all that sort of thing, and now here's another load of questions all bearing on the same thing. For example, 'Does an atom explosion which incinerates thousands of human bodies simultaneously cause pandemonium on the astral plane, or how does it affect or disturb them?'

It does not do a thing to harm them physically, but it certainly causes an awful flap because thousands of people are going to come to the astral world in one awful huddle. Many of them will be scared sick, many will be insane with shock, so all available helpers are rushed to help those who are pouring in and are in a very distressed state. The scene, actually, would be very much like that when there is a truly bad calamity on Earth such as an earthquake or something at least as disastrous where helpers and volunteer helpers rush to use any means possible to lend assistance. The answer then is nobody in the astral world is harmed by the detonation of the bomb, but they are very much upset by the extra work in trying to care for so many people all at one time because, while such an event will have been foreseen, yet all these 'foreseeings' are probabilities and not necessarily actual events which are just bound to occur.

The next one asks, 'How do the Manus of nations supervise the affairs of their nation? Do they work through the United Nations Representatives, through the heads of nations, their cabinets and advisers, or how?'

If the United Nations was as had been hoped, that would

have been the way for a Manu to work, but here is something that you have to consider very seriously, it may be distasteful to you, it may even be thoroughly shocking to you, but nevertheless it is actual fact.

This particular world is not a very advanced world, actually it is a penitentiary world, a hell, a hard school – call it what you will – and many of the Manus in charge of this world are themselves learning! As they gain experience and as they become successful, then, just like a departmental manager, they get promoted, and if the General Manager can make a success of things in his small branch then he might well be promoted to a much larger branch.

It really is necessary to look at things with an open mind and to remember that when on the Other Side in the astral one does not sit on a cloud and strum a banjo or pluck the strings of a harp; one has to work.

If you are in the kindergarten class at school you might think that the great big 'grown-ups' of twelve years of age in a class higher are real Gods who do nothing except tell the teachers where to go, and these twelve and fourteen year olds might think that the sixth-formers or thirteenth graders, or whatever you want to call them, are truly Gods of Creation. But these Gods of Creation still have to do homework, still have to attend classes, still have to gain experience. All right, people come to this Earth to gain experience, Manus look after this world (more or less) in order to gain experience, and if there are a few fights between countries, well, it's teaching humans and it's teaching Manus as well.

In higher states, that is, with much more advanced worlds, Manus can get together and discuss things amicably so that there are no wars and no particular crime, but that is much too advanced for the hoodlums of the Earth. The Earth people are here to learn the hard way because they won't learn in the soft way, the kind way. If a chap comes along and takes a swipe at you with a club or shows an earnest desire to bonk you on the noggin and lay you out, well, it's useless to say, 'I pray, my dear fellow, that you will

139

kindly desist from these unwelcome attentions.' Instead if you are wise you will kick him where it will do most harm, and then let out a hoot for the police.

So the Manus of this world are learners. They are learning things just as you are, and when they have learnt to straighten up things a bit they will move on to something better. But, cheer up, you have to stay only about seventy years or so to a lifetime, the poor Manus have a longer sentence than that by far.

Now here is a little question tucked in, 'It is understood that the line of the Thirteenth Dalai Lama was all the same soul. Could the Thirteenth be now in the Land of the Golden Light and still reincarnate in the Fourteenth?'

Well, that is the easiest question of all to answer because the Fourteenth Dalai Lama himself seems to have spilled the beans to the press and admitted that he is not a reincarnation of the Great Thirteenth, which is just as well because the Great Thirteenth is a very active entity indeed in the astral world doing very much good, and, I believe, rather sad that the present 'leaders' in exile in India are not doing much to aid suffering Tibet. But I dealt with that at some length in an earlier chapter of this book so perhaps I should not gild the lily or repeat myself when I need not.

Another person writes in referring to 'My Visit to Venus', but let me state here and now that I definitely, definitely, definitely do not recommend that 'book'. It is just a few pages containing some articles which I wrote years ago, and it contains some – well, I consider them off-beat – illustrations not done by me. This book containing parts of my work and filled out with a lot of blurb was published entirely without my permission and entirely against my wishes.

The same applies to a record, 'The Power of Prayer.' I definitely do not recommend it. The quality is exceedingly poor and it was never meant to be reproduced as a record. It is just something that I made many, many years ago, and when I left North America to go to South America I was informed that this record had been made without my permission, without my desire, during my absence from the continent.

If you want a real record then purchase the Meditation record which I made specially for a record. This was made specially to help people meditate, and it may be obtained from:–

Mr. E. Z. Sowter,
33 Ashby Road,
Loughborough,
Leicestershire,
England.

I will tell you that Mr. Sowter has world rights for this record and for Touch Stones and many other things, and he is the only person who has my full permission and agreement to sell my records and Touch Stones. He also sells various other things of my design.

That is a free advertisement for Mr. Sowter who is a very decent man and who is trying to do good.

This book is not meant to be a catalogue of nice people, it is not meant to be a catalogue of crummy dopes on the outer fringe of sanity either, but I cannot let the book be completed without mentioning a very pleasant family indeed: Mrs. Worstmann and her two daughters. You may recall that one of my books was dedicated to Mrs. Worstmann, a very pleasant, very highly educated woman whom it is a pleasure to know, and I have known her for several years, known her while her husband was still alive on this Earth, and I have been in touch with him now that he is on the Other Side. Mrs. Worstmann, then, is one of the more enlightened types. Certainly she was enlightened enough to have two talented daughters, Luise who is a nurse in one of the better London hospitals; she is a good nurse, but she is good at so many things. She is artistic – well, I am not going to list all her virtues, they are too many to put down on these pages. I want to mention, also, her sister, Therese, another talented one. She also is a nurse, and she is very anxious to train as a surgeon, she has all the capabilities for it, everything except the money in fact. I have been looking around to see if there were any Insurance Schemes which would enable a highly gifted young woman to get training as a surgeon. Unfortunately I have not yet found any such source, so if any of you, my Readers, know how to raise money whereby an entirely capable young woman can pay for her training at Medical School, then now is your chance to do good.

I make it clear, I make it absolutely clear, that this young lady has the ability to do some good for the world as a surgeon, and it seems rather dreadful that she may be deprived of the opportunity of doing that good through lack of money to finance her training.

Dealing with a surgeon-to-be, let us deal with heart transplants. I have a question here, 'What about the current rash of heart transplants and other radical surgery inserting foreign organs, plastic valves, and tubing, etc. into a body. From a purely material, physiological standpoint this seems to be considered an almost miraculous scientific breakthrough, but does it do the trick? Will the use of various chemicals counteract the normal tendency of the body to reject any foreign material introduced into it this way? Or is such rejection inevitable simply because the substituting of a healthy new organ into a body to replace a diseased member, won't result in proper meshing between the still diseased etheric of the organ in question with the artificially introduced material counterpart? And, furthermore, is there anything really gained for the individual being operated upon if he has a few months or even years of invalidism added to his present stay on Earth, unless he really uses the time gained thereby to learn some really worthwhile lessons which would otherwise have been deferred to another incarnation?'

Well, that's a mouthful, certainly! Many hundreds of centuries ago in the days of Atlantis people could do transplants. It was possible in those days to graft on an arm or a leg, possible to replace hearts and kidneys and lungs, but it was a providential act of Nature that a civilization which did such things came to an end. They tried replacing brains, and they produced amoral monsters.

Basically there is nothing very difficult in replacing a heart. It is just a mechanical procedure. You have to cut out the heart and you have to trim the replacement heart to exactly fit the 'pipes' which are left. Any competent surgeon could do such an operation.

In the physical world one has a semi-invalid. After all, when one does such a radical operation certain small blood vessels and nerves cannot be rejoined, the whole structure becomes impaired and so a very sick man is given an added sickness – impairment of his body. But still such a person could go on for an indefinite number of years, go on living a life of semi-invalidism.

In the astral world, however, there are two people who are suffering greatly by being 'cross-mixed'. One person is half in the astral, that is, he goes to the astral world during sleep only, and the other person is right in the astral but because his heart or other organ is still living he has a sort of sympathetic attachment through the Silver Cord of the person who now has that organ.

You sometimes get two radios; you switch on two radios in the same room, perhaps on the same programme, and if you switch off one then it does make slightly more volume to the second, there is some interaction between the two, and these are only radios, only things which some set of girls put together while they were talking about their latest boy friends and how mini their mini skirts would be the next season. When you get to living humans the interaction is much, much stronger, and it definitely, very definitely, impairs the efficiency of a person living in the astral world to be even 'sympathetically' connected to the body of another person.

It is my firm belief that replacing organs like this is terribly, criminally wrong, and really people should not permit such abuses of Nature. The reflections from the donor's heart show up in the aura of the recipient, and the two people may not have been compatible. The fact that one could be coloured and the other white has nothing to do with it. The basic rate of vibration, that is, the frequency of each person, has everything to do with it, and I certainly hope that such transplants can be outlawed.

It is a different matter if one is replacing an organ with a synthetic organ because that is no worse than a person wearing glasses or a hearing aid or clothing, no worse than using a crutch.

I believe that medical scientists should be encouraged to devise artificial organs which could safely be used on humans, then there would be no cross-linkage between two entities which causes a handicap to both entities until both are free of their Silver Cords and living in the astral world. So, to answer this specific question, I am definitely opposed to organ transplants.

Here is another question which should be of general interest. It is:–

'Information or directions on how a few people working devotedly could bring about a change in the course of world affairs.'

If a few people would definitely think 'in step' on a specific subject, then whatever they think about could actually be so. Nowadays people cannot hold a thought for more than a second or two. If you doubt that, try it yourself, try and think about one specific subject while watching the seconds hand of your watch. You will find, if you are honest, that your attention will waver and wander far more rapidly than you would believe possible. Your attention will only stay more or less constant if you are thinking about something to do with yourself, something you want, something you want to do, something which affects you deeply. Anything else such as bringing help to another person whom you have met – well, you cannot hold the interest for very long.

Peoples' thought is not constant, and no one thinks of the

same thing at the same time with the same intensity. They are like a mass of people milling about, all walking but all out of step, whereas if people could think 'in step' then they could indeed accomplish miracles. If you want to think of this further, consider an army of men, consider a regiment of soldiers marching over a bridge. If those men marched in step across the bridge they would destroy it, and for that reason the men are instructed before going on to the bridge to 'break step'. So they go over walking just as a disorderly rabble would walk, not in step, not in rhythm, and so the building up effect of many men walking in step is destroyed, there isn't the force there any longer, and the bridge is not damaged.

If you could get a number of men marching absolutely in step they would destroy any bridge that could be made, and if one kept up the marching they could destroy a building also because the constant pounding down and lifting up would build up such a series of vibrations that the amplitude or degree of vibration would increase and increase beyond the point where the natural elasticity of the bridge or building could encompass it, and then the bridge would just shatter like a broken glass.

If one could get – oh, half a dozen people, and get them to think definitely, deliberately in waves of the correct pattern they could topple governments, or build governments, they could make one country pre-eminent over all others, and they could do things which now would be regarded as utterly impossible.

It is perhaps fortunate that it is not too easy to get people to think in unison at exactly the right frequency because, and I am telling you this quite seriously, it is not a joke, if one had a gang of crooks who were trained in thinking correctly they could think open a bank vault. Dear me, what a pity I haven't a nice little gang; it would be very pleasant to have a nice load of money, wouldn't it? Still, it is truly quite possible, and in fact in Atlantean days it was an everyday occurrence.

The Catholic chants are a relic of those bygone days, chants which some think are only two thousand years old, but they are still chants which have been built on the original songs of power of the Sumerians and the Atlanteans. Perhaps I should put it the other way round, Atlanteans and Sumerians because, of course, the Atlanteans are the oldest civilization of the two.

In those days it was possible to lift massive chunks of stone by thought, by having a trained mass of priests thinking at the same time under their conductor so that the stone would lift straight up in the air.

If you think that is too fantastic remember that you can make a sound which will break a glass. If you sustain the sound you can break a glass or break a window, and thought is just another form of sound, that is, a vibration, everything is a vibration, and if you set the right vibration in motion you can accomplish anything.

Another question; 'Readers are wondering when will be the proper time for the free world to know of the Time Capsules.'

The proper time is not yet. The proper time is not until the end of this civilization, the end of this civilization as we know it at present. Later – oh, not in your lifetime, so don't worry: – much later there will be earthquakes which will really shake the crust of the Earth and these Time Capsules will be thrown up to the surface ready to be opened. There are quite a number of them. One tremendous capsule is in Egypt; I suppose technically it is a capsule, but actually it is a vast chamber deep beneath the shifting sands of the Egyptian Desert. The Chamber is an absolute museum of artefacts which existed tens of thousands of years ago – yes, 'tens of thousands of years ago'.

There are aircraft of a very very different type than those in use now, aircraft which work by anti-gravity so that the power of the motor is not expended in supporting the weight but is used just to propel the vehicle forward. I will tell you quite truthfully that I have seen such an aircraft.

146

One device would be especially of interest to the house-wife or to the person who has to carry weights. It is a sort of handle which attaches to whatever has to be carried, and then one just catches hold of the handle as when one is carrying a basket. If the parcel or bundle is heavy then the handle is depressed more, if the parcel is not very heavy then the handle is not very far depressed. Each of these devices was constructed so that no matter whether the parcel weighed a ton or ten pounds, the person had no more than about a pound of effort to expend.

Anti-gravity was a perfectly ordinary, perfectly common thing in centuries long past, but the priests of that day, who also were the leaders of the armies, got a bit cross with each other, and each side tried bigger and better weapons than the other, with the result that they blew their whole civilization in the air, and it came down as a radio-active dust.

Later, when these Time Capsules are opened, television in three dimensions will be seen, and not just 3-D by means of two cameras or two lens, but a thing in which there appear to be actual people, miniature size, of course, acting out plays, dances, and even debates.

Photography too was different in those days, there were no such things as the flat photographs which we now see. Everything was in the 'solid', more 3-D than 3-D itself. The nearest thing is the very, very crude holograms with which scientists are just experimenting in which you can almost look behind the object you had photographed. Well, in the days of Atlantis you could look behind!

Hundreds of centuries ago there was the mightiest civilization the world had seen up to that time, but there was such a cataclysm that people became almost demented, those that were left, and they had to start just about from the savage state and the present so-called Age of Science has barely reached what would be called the kindergarten stage when Atlantis was at its peak.

Many people disbelieve in Atlantis which, of course, is just utterly foolish. They are like the fishermen who go out fishing and because they don't catch anything they say, 'Oh, there are no fish in the seas any more, they have all died off.'

Yes, there was an Atlantis, and there are living remnants of Atlantis still, deep underground in a certain part of the world, and let me make clear here that that part of the world is *not* Mount Shasta. Don't believe all the hooey you read or are told about Mount Shasta; this is just an ordinary area which has been over publicized by people who wanted to make not just a fast buck, but a whole sack of them.

I wish I could tell you some of the things I absolutely, definitely *know*, but there are certain things which cannot be told at present. I know the actual truth about the submarines *Thresher* and *Scorpion*, and I know what happened to them and why. The story, if it could be told, would make cold chills run up and down your spine, but the time is not yet. There are many things which could be told, but – well – these books circulate everywhere, many, many people read them, and there are many people who should not be aware that certain people know what is really going on. You can take it, though, that the mystery of the *Thresher* and the *Scorpion* is a stranger thing than you would ever believe.

'But you seem so very interested in animals,' said the letter, 'and yet you say that you do not believe in vegetarianism. Why? How do you reconcile the two, a love of animals and a dislike of vegetarianism?'

I believe most firmly that Man has a body which at this stage of existence needs meat for its sustenance. Now, let me tell you something. Countless years ago – years and years and years ago – there was a form of Man who was entirely a vegetarian. He was so busy eating that he had no time for anything else. It never occurred to him to eat meat, and so that he could deal with the tremendous bulk of vegetables, fruit and nuts necessary he had an additional organ, the last vestigal remnant of which is the appendix.

The experiment was a complete failure. The Gardeners of the Earth found that vegetarian Man was inefficient because to take in the necessary amount of cellulose matter to enable him to do any worthwhile work was quite a prohibitive matter. He would have to be eating all the time, eating for so long that there would not be any time left for him to do any constructive work. And so the Gardeners of the Earth scrapped that type of Man, or, if you don't like the word 'scrapped,' let us say that through evolution mankind turned into a meat-eater.

We have to face basic facts, and one of the basic facts is this; all vegetable matter is cellulose supported. Now, you imagine lace curtains, a nice openwork net, and then you stuff the holes with paste stuff containing food substance. Supposing you had to eat the lace curtains in order that the food value packed in the holes could be absorbed into your body. It sounds a bit fantastic, doesn't it? But that's just what you do when you eat a lot of lettuce or cabbage or other vegetable or fruit stuff. What you are eating is a cellulose sponge, the holes of which are packed with food, but the sponge material takes up a lot of room and so to get an adequate amount of food one has to take a quite excessive bulk of cellulose, and the poor wretched body cannot digest cellulose, you know, it has to be excreted.

In all my life I have never, never met a vegetarian who could do any hard work. Of course if he was sitting on his behind all day letting other people do the work, then no doubt he could get by, but he wouldn't be very bright. If by any chance he was bright then you could take it that if he lived naturally he would be a darn sight brighter.

Quite truly have you ever seen a navvy or a person who does hard manual work who could live on vegetables and fruits only? You haven't have you, now you come to think of it?

But let us get back to our animal business. I am truly an animal lover, I love all animals, and I can assure you that animals know they have to die sometime and it helps their own kharma if they can die for a useful purpose.

Animals who are raised for food are looked after, they are

bred carefully, any sickness is treated. The herd is very carefully supervised so that there are only healthy animals.

In the wild state you get animals who are diseased or stunted, or who have been injured in some way, or even those who have some disease such as cancer or lung trouble and they just have to drag out a miserable existence. Supposing an animal breaks a leg, then it has to live out a really miserable existence until it dies in pain and starvation, yet any herd animal would be cared for immediately.

If no one killed any animals then soon the world would be overrun with animals of every type. There would be cattle in large numbers, and the greater the number of cattle then the greater the number of predator animals which Nature herself would provide to keep down the number of cattle.

If humans eat meat, then it's to their advantage to kill an animal painlessly and quickly. In killing an animal for food one is also keeping down the numbers of animals and keeping them in check so that in growing to uncontrollable numbers and in running wild the stock does not become downgraded.

Now whether we like it or not, humans also have to be kept in check so far as their numbers are concerned. If there are too many humans then inevitably there is a big war or a serious earthquake, or some sort of plague or illness which carries off large numbers of humans. That is just the Gardeners of the Earth thinning out the ranks, cutting down on surplus people; people, after all, are just animals of a different type.

And all the people who fairly yowl with anguish at the thought of a person eating a piece of beef, well, how about eating a live lettuce? If one eats a piece of beef or chicken the original owner of the flesh is no longer able to feel the bites, yet people go and eat live lettuce, eat live pears, so how do they reconcile their so-called humanitarian principles?

Science, cynical and sceptical though it be, has now discovered that plants have feelings, plants will grow better when they are tended by people who are sympathetic to them. Plants respond to music. There are instruments which can indicate how much pain a plant is enduring. You may not hear a cabbage shriek when you tear off its outside leaves – no, because it has no vocal chords and yet there are instruments which can record that shriek of pain as a burst of static.

This is not fairy tale stuff, it's actual fact, it's stuff that has been investigated and proved and proved again. In research laboratories in Russia, England and the U.S.A. it has been proved.

When you pick some berries and stuff them in your mouth, well how about the feelings of the plant? You don't go and tear a lump off a cow and stuff it in your mouth do you? If you tried to the cow would soon object, but because a plant cannot make its pain known you think you are a jolly wonderful humanitarian when you eat plants instead of meat which cannot feel the pain of being eaten.

Quite frankly I believe that vegetarians are a lot of cranks and crackpots, and if they would only come off their stupid attitudes and remember that the Gardeners of the Earth designed their bodies for certain food, then they would be a lot better in their mental health.

If you have a car you wouldn't drain the sump and fill it up with water, would you, and say you couldn't possibly use oil because it might come from the Earth somewhere and hurt somebody underground. If you try to run your body on food for which it is not designed you are being just the same as a person who won't use oil in the sump of his car but instead uses salt water.

If we are going to be logical and if we are going to say that vegetarianism is good, then how about the practice of using cut flowers in one's rooms? Plants are living entities, and when you cut flowers you are cutting off the sex organs of the plants and sticking them in vases, and actually humans would be shockingly unhappy if their sex organs were cut off and stuck in cases for some different race to enjoy.

Let me digress here to say that when I was in hospital I

received a very pleasant surprise. A group of very kind ladies as far away as the Pacific coast of the U.S.A. had wired to a florist in the city of Saint John to have some plants delivered to me at the hospital. I appreciated it very much indeed. The ladies did not give any address but I was able to locate them!

A personal choice – I do not like cut flowers. It seems to me such a pity to cut them off. Instead I very much prefer a complete plant, here one has a living thing which is growing and not just dying. I often think people who send great bunches of cut flowers – well, why not cut off the heads of small children and impale them on sticks and put those in a room!

Have you ever thought of the state this old Earth of ours is in? It's quite a mess, you know. Compare it to a garden. Now, if the garden is properly maintained there are no weeds or anything like that, all pests are kept in check, there is no blight on the trees and the fruits are full and healthy.

Plants have to be thinned out, the sickly ones have to be removed. Every so often fruit trees have to be pruned, sometimes there are grafts taken. It is necessary to carefully supervise the garden and to prvent cross-pollination between undesirable species. If the garden is maintained as it should be it becomes a thing of beauty.

But let the gardeners go away, let the garden remain idle for a year or two. Weeds will grow and will choke and kill off the more delicate plants, unchecked pests will come, and blight will appear on the trees. No longer will there be round, firm fruits, but soon they will be shrivelled, wrinkled up with all sorts of brown spots. A sadly neglected garden is a tragic sight.

Or let us go from the garden to livestock. Have you ever seen wild ponies on a moor, or wild cattle where the grazing is poor? They become stunted, some of them suffer from rickets, many suffer from skin diseases. Generally they are a pretty pathetic sight, little dwarf creatures, unkempt and very, very wild.

Look at a well maintained stock yard. Here you see pedigree animals carefully bred, faults bred out of them in fact. You get fine pedigree horses or excellent pedigree cows; they are healthy, they are large and substantial looking, they appear glad to be alive, and you can look at them with pleasure knowing that they are not going to start away from you in fright. They know they are looked after.

Now think of the Earth, think of the people here. The stock is getting poorer and poorer. People are becoming more vicious, people are listening to more depraved 'music' and watching ever more obscene pictures. Now it is no longer an age when beauty and spirituality count, no longer do people love good music, love good pictures, everything is being torn down. You cannot get a great man without some moronic clot trying to say unkind things about him. One of the greatest men of modern times, Sir Winston Churchill, probably saved the world from being under the cloud of Communism, yet even Sir Winston Churchill had his detractors just because of the spirit of evil which pervades the atmosphere nowadays.

The garden which is the Earth which is our world has gone to seed. Weeds grow apace. You can see them in the streets with their long hair and dirty complexions, and if you can't see them you can jolly well smell them yards off.

The races need pruning, stock needs replenishing and soon will come the time when the Gardeners of the Earth come back for their periodical inspection and find conditions here to be quite intolerable.

Something will be done about it. Mankind will not be left to go to bad seed as it has of late. There will come a time when all the Races of Man will unite, when there will no longer be black people and white people and yellow people and red people, the whole world will be peopled by 'the Race of Tan', and that will be the predominating colour – tan.

With the coming of the Race of Tan there will be much fresh life injected in the human race. People will again value the better things of life, people will again value spiritual

153

things and when mankind gets spiritual to a sufficient degree it will be possible for mankind once again to talk by telepathy with 'the Gods' – the Gardeners of the Earth.

At present Man has sunk in the slough of despond, sunk in his own lack of spirituality, sunk so low that his basic vibrations are reduced to such an extent that he cannot be heard telepathically by any creature higher, not even by his fellows. But the time will come when all that will be remedied.

I am not trying to sell you Buddhism, nor Christianity, nor Judaism, but I am saying quite definitely that there will have to be a return to some form of religion because only religion can give one the necessary spiritual discipline which will convert an unholy rabble of humanity to a disciplined spiritual group of people, who can carry on the race instead of having it ploughed under and a fresh set of entities placed here.

Now, in the present state of dissonance, even Christians fight against Christians. The war in Northern Ireland between Catholics and Protestants – it doesn't matter who is right or who is wrong, they are both alleged to be Christians, they are both alleged to follow the same religion. Does it matter whether one sect crosses himself with the left hand while another does it with the right hand? It's much the same as one of the stories in Gulliver's Travels where the people of one mythical country went to war about which end of an egg should be opened first, the small end or the broad end! How can Christianity possibly try to convert other nations, other religions, when Christians fight against Christians, because both Catholics and Protestants are Christians.

CHAPTER TEN

The gem cannot be polished
without friction, nor Man
perfected without trials.

BREAKFAST was soon over. One doesn't take long to con-
sume a breakfast consisting solely of one fifty gram boiled
egg, one piece of bread, and five grams of butter. The two
cups of tea permitted did not take long 'going down the
hatch' either.

The Old Man pressed the button on the left-hand side of
the bed and a motor whirred, and the back section lifted up
to a forty-five degree inclination. 'Oh!' smiled Cleo, 'I
do love it when that thing goes up.'

'Well, I have to work now, and you wretches mustn't disturb me again. You know what fun we had yesterday, don't
you?'

The end of Miss Cleo's tail twitched with amusement, and
she sauntered off to her accustomed place on the windowsill
right over the radiator.

'What fun yesterday?' asked Ra'ab. 'I don't remember any
fun yesterday.'

The Old Man looked up and said, 'I tried to do some of
the book in the afternoon, and Fat Cat Taddy said I mustn't
do it. She said I didn't look well enough and when I
wouldn't stop she told me again and then she kept jumping
at me and slapping me.'

'Good for her,' said Ra'ab, 'she's just looking after you.'

'Yes, sure she's looking after me, but she kept on jumping
at me and trying to push things out of the way, she tried to
sit on my chest so I couldn't work, and if I don't get on and
do this book who is going to pay all the doctor's bills?'

The Old Man thought with considerable gloom of all the people still making money out of him; Secker & Warburg, for instance, first published *The Third Eye* – oh, about fifteen years ago, they published it in hardback form and then they sold the rights to a paperback firm, and ever since Secker & Warburg have been taking fifty per cent of the royalties on the paperback edition. And the same thing happens with Doubleday in the U.S.A. There are other publishers who are dipping their hands in and, as the Old Man said, it's no wonder he never had any money when there were so many people, including the tax collectors, who were trying to get a share of the money that he earned.

The Old Man thought always in the kindest of terms about Corgi of England because throughout a long association there has never been any disagreement, never one word of dispute between Corgi and him. He thought with considerable affection of his Agent, Mr. A. S. Knight of the firm of Stephen Aske, a painfully honest man who has always done his best and, as stated, the Old Man had a considerable affection for him. That all came about because a former Agent with whom the Old Man was dealing said, 'If you know of a better Agent, find him.' And the Old Man did just that – Mr. Knight.

But now was the time to work once again, the time to pass on a few more bits of information to people who would appreciate it. The Old Man turned over his papers and Fat Cat Taddy raised her head and glowered, and sent the strong telepathic message, 'No larks now, you cannot do too much at once or this time Cleo and I will both jump at you.' Having said that she curled up comfortably and awaited further developments.

Quite a lot of questions came to the Old Man, quite a lot of letters. People wanting things, wanting help, wanting suggestions, but most of the people wanted the Old Man to agree with them so they would be justified in their own minds. So many people wrote in about love affairs, asking the Old Man to decide between that person or some other person, asking if they would be happily married, and all the rest of it, but most of the people did not want any advice that meant doing anything, they just wanted to be told that they were doing satisfactorily and needn't make any more effort, they wanted to be told that fate was too hard on them and that they were worthy of the deepest sympathy and just give up and don't do anything, you can't fight against fate. You can, you know, if you want to.

People come to Earth with a very carefully worked out plan of what they are going to do. They are fired with enthusiasm and determination, they know exactly how successful they are going to be in the forthcoming life. So they set out on the journey to Earth like Crusaders full of zeal. When they get down to Earth, and when they have a few years experience behind them, inertia or lethargy sets in, they get disillusioned with life which is a more polite way of saying downright lazy, which is actually the truth. People try to evade their responsibilities, try to shirk the plan which they, and they only approved because, remember, nothing is forced upon a person, a person comes to learn certain things, to experience certain things, but they are not made to. In the same way a student who goes to a University – well, he didn't have to go, he doesn't have to learn certain things unless he wants to. If he doesn't learn then he won't get the desired qualifications and that's all there is to it; it's his choice.

People ask for advice and guidance, they absolutely vow that they will follow the advice, but then they go on in their most erratic way, a way that is something like trying to drive a pig to market. Have you ever driven a pig to market? No? Well, it's like this; you have two long sticks in your hands and you get behind the pig, and then you try to drive him forward in a straight line and the stick in each hand is to give him a little tap if he doesn't keep to the prescribed course. Nowadays, of course, pigs get driven in trucks to market which is altogether too easy, but people try to do everything except the obvious. People cannot understand that the Path is here, right beside them, right in front of them, the Path is within reach. People won't believe that, they think they have to travel to some exotic country and seek the Path there, they think they have to go to Tibet and get a Guide, or become a Buddhist. The number of people who claim they have Tibetan Lamas as Guides – well, there just isn't the population in Tibet. And the number of people who write to me and tell me that they are going to Tibet to study in a Lamasery indicates that so few people really read the Truth; they can't go to Tibet, the Communists are there, the Lamaseries are closed. It's just silly to think that because a person is all fired up with enthusiasm that he can go charging off leaping across the oceans and landing with a plonk in Darjeeling, and then making his way on an outstretched red carpet to the nearest Lamasery. What do you think the Communists are there for? They are there to stop religion, they are there to kill off lamas, they are there to enslave innocent people, and they are doing it because there doesn't seem to be anybody who is going to lead the Tibetan people out of the wilderness, out of the darkness of Communism and into the light (such as it is) of the free world.

It should be emphasized once again that if people seek advice and receive advice, and then ignore advice, then they are much worse off than if they did not seek help in the first case because when the Path is pointed out to them, when they are told what they really should do after having invited suggestions, then, well, they add a bit more to their kharma if they do not do it. So if you do not want to do anything about your state, about your dissatisfaction, do not seek advice, otherwise you are just adding on a bit to your own load.

Now here is another question; 'The idea has been gleaned that efforts to bring about healing of the sick may be ill-advised, interfering with the kharma the patient is working off, and such helper may be subsequently burdened with the patient's kharma. If this was true, what about the practising physician, what a load of kharma he must get. Is one supposed to try and help and heal or not?'

Poor old kharma takes a beating once again! Not everything is due to kharma, you know. People tell me that I must have a terrible kharma to have such a difficult life, but it's not that at all. For example, if you go out and do some hard work, dig a ditch or run a mile, that may be hardship to some people but you may be doing it because you like it or because you are studying something. You may dig a ditch to see if you can discover some better way of doing it.

Many people come to this Earth with a definite plan that they will have a specific illness, it might be T.B., it might be cancer, it might even be chronic headache. No matter what it is, that person can come with a definite plan to have some definite illness. A person may come as a mentally sick person and be doing an extremely good job of studying mentally sick people. It doesn't at all mean that because a person is mentally sick that they are burdened down with kharma; on the contrary, they may be coming so that they can study at first hand mentally sick people and then when they return to the Other Side they can help through the astral world those who are sick upon the Earth.

A physician or surgeon is in a special category. He can help those who need to be helped, he can operate on those who otherwise would die, and the sufferer, if he or she came with the intention of studying illness, would be able to study how the suffering of such illness may be alleviated.

Let me make this statement; so-called 'faith healers' do tremendous harm by setting up conflicting vibrations. The faith healer may be full of good intentions, but then the road to Hell is paved with good intentions, people say, and unless the faith healer knows the exact cause of an illness it is definitely, definitely harmful to start up all this so-called healing business. It just sets up a jangle in the aura which, all too frequently, makes the condition worse.

In these 'miracle cure' cases it is sadly all too frequent that the person did not have the illness in the first case, but merely had a neurosis. Some people can delude themselves for years, they can go into a state of auto-hypnosis – yes, they've got cancer, yes, they've got T.B., yes, they've got everything. They can go to a doctor's waiting room, hear a few other patients discussing their symptoms, and then the neurotic person copies the whole bunch and gets one 'illness' after another. Now, if a faith healer can come along and 'cure' that, often there is a serious breakdown after it. Quite frankly I have no time and no patience with these faith healers.

If you are ill go to a recognized doctor. If you need other specialized attention a qualified doctor will advise it and tell you where and how to get it, but to just send a sum of money to somebody who advertises in the *Tom Cat Times* about faith healing – well, that really is insane.

A recognized doctor naturally does not add to his kharma in helping to cure the sick. This business of kharma is so dreadfully misunderstood. It doesn't at all mean that if you are going to help a person you are going to take all his hardships on to your own back. It means that if you do an ill service to a person, then you have to pay back. If, through your viciousness, or your violent temper let us say, you shoot a person and impede the accomplishment of the task which he was doing, then you have to pay by having your own path impeded. Forget about hellfire and damnation because there is no such thing, no one is ever, ever abandoned, no one is ever, ever condemned to torments. The only suffering and torment that you will experience when you leave this Earth is when you enter the Hall of Memories and see what stupid things you have done, and that is easily overcome; if you really do your best now while you are still upon Earth, you can be assured that your visit to the Hall of Memories will not be so bad after all. Of course your face will be red, but – well, no wonder, eh? Think of some of the things you have done, think of some of the things you haven't done.

Here is a question about telepathy. 'Could more detail be given regarding the means of reaching the octave for telepathy between animals and Man. How can cat wavelengths be intercepted, for instance?'

If you want to talk telepathically with animals you have

to be in complete rapport with those animals, you have to be able to think as they do, you have to love them, and you have to treat them as equals. Most people regard animals as some inferior species of life, they think of animals as dumb clucks or dumb creatures who just cannot speak and, therefore, haven't any brains. Let me tell you that many humans think that deaf humans are mentally bereft. If you had ever been deaf, or if people thought you were deaf, you would often hear them discussing you, saying, 'Oh, he's a bit weak in the head, he doesn't know what we're saying, don't bother with him.'

Animals are in every way the equal of the human animal, they are just in a different shape, they think along different lines, and because they think along different lines their basic wavelength is different.

But let me give you another cause for thought; can you telepathise with a fellow human? No? Do you know why? Throughout the years humans have distrusted humans, humans try to conceal their actions from humans. There is always more or less the intent of deceiving fellow humans, so you try sub-consciously to make the wavelength of your thought transmission at variance with the thought transmission of other humans then they can't pick up your thoughts. If there was true 'brotherly love' on this Earth everyone would be telepathic to each other. It is only humans who are not telepathic, or rather, only humans who cannot use telepathic ability.

I speak to my cats quite as distinctly, quite as easily as I speak to any human. I speak to that Big Fat Cat Taddykins and she gets my message with absolute clarity and I receive her reply, and often the Beauty Queen Cleo will come rushing out of another room so that she can take part in any discussion. Womanlike she likes to have the last word.

If you want to talk telepathically with animals you have to love them, you have to treat them as an equal, you have to realize that they think rather differently from humans but they are no less intelligent because of that.

An Englishman and a Spaniard construct their sentences

differently, but then so do a German and a Frenchman. The basic message is the same, but the actual construction is different. It is even more so between human and cat. You also have to take into consideration that the cat's viewpoint of things is different from that of a human. So unless you can think as a cat much of the messages you would receive would be somewhat incomprehensible to you. As an illustration, I was given a message about something I wanted – this was when I lived in Montreal. I got an actual picture of the shop where the article was for sale, but, of course, the picture was from a cat's-eyeview of a few inches from the ground, and from that peculiar angle I just could not get the name of the shop because of the extreme elongation of the letters of the name seen from near-ground level. Only when the cat, specially to oblige me, jumped on top of a car could I actually read the name through the cat's eyes. Yes, I got the article and it was quite satisfactory.

There are many such instances. I wanted something for research and no shop could supply me, so Miss Taddy, our highly gifted telepathic cat, sent out a general call on the cats' telepathic wavelength and we received the desired information from a French-Canadian cat. So here in New Brunswick we have received a message from a cat in the Province of Quebec, and an urgent telephone call really truly did locate the thing that I wanted. I had no idea where to get it, but by contacting cats I was soon in possession of the article.

I have a friend living many thousands of miles away and through receiving telepathic messages he has been saved much trouble. Miss Taddy was in touch telepathically with a cat who lives near my friend, and this cat who was quite a good telepath himself was able to inform Taddy of certain things. Then I got in touch with my friend and gave him the information, and he confirmed that everything was actually as I said.

If people would practise telepathy they could soon put the telephone companies out of business. Perhaps you and I should get together and set up a special telepathic telephone communications system and make ourselves rich!

Here is another question which possibly is a little belated and, like most other things in this book, will be out of place. Before I say about the question let me say something else:–

In this book I have deliberately had questions 'higgly-piggly', otherwise too many people would just run to that question in which they were interested, or that section in which they were interested, and ignore the rest of the book. They would then write and complain to me that I had not dealt with such-and-such a thing which they had not read because they forgot to turn the page:

Here is the question; 'It is the spirit that survives, isn't it? Now when a person has a mental affliction does that mean that it is more than a physical impairment, something that will not be left behind when we pass into another existence, or will a person automatically be free of it as soon as the spirit gets out of the body, just as one wouldn't feel a broken leg, for instance, on the astral plane.'

Many people come down here with a deliberate mental affliction. They come down to see at firsthand what it is like to be mentally impaired. It doesn't mean that their kharma is faulty at all, that is nothing to do with it. You might say that a horse who has a handicap in a race has kharma, and that would be absurd, wouldn't it?

In some races I understand that horses who are consistent winners have a handicap in that they have to carry certain weights which are assumed to slow them up a bit and give other horses a chance. Mind you, I know very little about horses, I have never yet found the brake pedal on a horse, but I do know which is the front end and which is the rear end. The front end bites and one also has to avoid the rear end for various other reasons which we need not detail.

No horse would be accused of having kharma when it carries handicap weights. In the same way no human would be accused of having kharma when he or she comes to this

163

Earth with a deliberate derangement or malfunction of some organ, and if a person should come here as a raving lunatic that would have no effect whatsoever on the astral body. The insane part is shed when the astral body 'goes home'.

In addition to the class of person who comes with a deliberate affliction that he may study the matter, there are those who, through mischance, are injured perhaps through a mother having a faulty diet, or possibly through a midwife or doctor using instruments in a faulty manner. For an illustration let us say that a doctor uses instruments and damages the skull, then the person may have a definite mental impairment as a result of that damage. But it's not necessarily the person's kharma 'paying him back'. It could be an accident, a mischance, and nothing more. Nor does it mean that the poor wretched doctor has got a load of kharma added because some things are accidents, and it does not mean that if a person has a definite, unavoidable accident, he is going to be saddled with kharma. There is such a lot of misconception about kharma.

The person who comes down and is injured through a complete mischance gets 'credits' because the failure of that life was not of his making. If he is very badly impaired, that is, if he is what we term a human vegetable, then the astral itself will go and take up residence elsewhere, and the human vegetable will then continue to tick over throughout the rest of the life, getting neither better nor worse.

There is no way known on Earth whereby an action on Earth can make an astral entity insane. The nearest one can come to it is when one takes drugs excessively. If one takes drugs to excess, then the astral entity is very definitely affected, not to the extent of being violently insane of course, but it does cause a bad nervous condition, and that has to be cured by quite a long sojourn in an astral hospital.

Much the same conditions prevail when a person is a real out and out alcoholic because through his drunkenness he has loosened the bonds between the astral and the physical and has actively encouraged lower grade elementals to

164

attack the Silver Cord, or even to take over the physical body completely. This causes a very severe shock to the astral and, again, while it does not cause insanity it does cause shock. The shock is akin to that which you would experience if you were asleep and a whole gang of rowdy kids beating drums and sounding trumpets jumped on your bed, not just appeared in your room, but actually jumped on your bed. You would suffer a severe shock, your skin would become pallid, your heart would race and you would get palpitations, and generally you would begin to shake all over. Well, when you had beaten up the kids and tossed them out you would be perhaps an hour or two before you fully recovered. But if your astral body had got into this condition through an alcoholic state or through excessive taking of drugs, you might be several years in the astral recovering from it.

That brings me to another question which is, 'What is this about powers that live on the astral plane at times affecting the Silver Cord'?

Let us visualize the prevailing conditions. Suppose we were sitting on top of a building, perhaps in a very beautiful pent house, with a nice roof garden; we were lolling at ease but at the same time keeping contact with a person right down on the ground level, we were keeping contact through, if you like, a pair of telephone wires connected to a headset on us and a headset and mouthpiece on the person right down on the ground floor. We are picking up his impressions and listening in to all that he says and hears. Our telephone wires are such that they can pass through trees and walls without being disturbed, but they can be disturbed by a certain type of entity.

Down below, also, there is a gang of hoodlum kids, yelling whooping around. They keep on trying to catch this telephone cable, and when they do catch it they try to break it or even lay it on a stone on the ground and give some hearty bashes at it with another stone. Although they cannot break it, they can cause considerable bruising and disturbance. It also impedes the poor wretch who is trying to talk and move about.

Now let us put it in astral terms. We are down here on the Earth – unfortunately – and our Silver Cord stretches upwards to the astral world. If we are weak or afraid, that is, if our authority is not respected, then any low grade elemental through whose territory our Silver Cord passes can take a grab at it and do to it, or try to do to it, much the same as the children on Earth tried to do to the telephone wires. Perhaps they cannot actually touch it, but they can impress signals upon it by magnetic induction in just the same way as one can speak into a microphone attached to a tape recorder and our messages spoken into the microphone are magnetically impressed on the tape which is passing through the recording head. Now supposing we are making a tape recording; we are busy doing our best diction, making our best composition, and we are quite proud of the job we are making, and then someone sneaks up behind us and shouts 'BOO!' into the microphone. It causes a disturbance, it shakes us considerably, and it leads to irritation on the person's part when listening to the recording.

If children respect one – and for that one has to really scare the daylights out of them – they will not do such things as to try and shout into microphones, etc. In the same way, one must absolutely and utterly show that one is not a bit afraid of the elementals. The elementals work hard at trying to make astral travelling humans afraid of them, they blow themselves out, they put on their fiercest looks and they utter the most outlandish cries one can imagine. Actually, the lower astral, the world of the elementals, is very much like the really insane ward at the local hospital. However, provided one maintains discipline, and it's easy, and provided that one is not afraid of these stupid elementals, and that is easier still, then there is never any cause to worry about interference from astral entities. Remember that nothing whatever can upset you or disturb you or hurt you unless you are terrified. If you are terrified, then your own state of fright, and that only, will cause your chemicals to be upset. If a person receives a bad fright it upsets one's digestion in the physical, and – well, that's all there is to it; you really cannot be hurt, but you cannot be even disturbed if you refuse to be frightened or intimidated.

Now here is a question which was asked by a mother. The question is, 'When children go to the Other Side do they grow up or do they stay as children? How do the parents know their child? Do they grow before their eyes?'

Mother, no, I won't mention your name because I did not ask you in time, and I will not mention any name except with the person's actual permission. So – Mother, you've got it all wrong. Now read this carefully; people are on the Other Side, that is, in the astral. They are not children, and they are not old people, they are of just what one might term an average, indeterminate age, because on the Other Side years are different. But, anyway, this person, an adult let us say, decides to go back to Earth; he cannot go back as a fully grown adult, can he? He has to go through the usual channels, one might say, and so this person goes to sleep and when he wakes up he is in the process of being born as a baby.

Then he grows a bit and, let us for the purpose of this illustration say that, when he is – oh, what shall we say? – when he is ten years of age he dies and is buried. The astral is released from the body and goes back to the Other Side where he says, in effect, 'Well, that was a short stay, thank goodness. Now what do I do next?' On the Other Side he is not a child any longer, but supposing that for some very, very important reason he has to get in touch with those who were his parents on Earth, it would be no good giving them the impression of himself as an adult, as one perhaps older than the parents. So he impresses upon their sub-conscious sight a vision of himself as a child, and the fond parents rejoice at having seen the spirit of their ten year old boy who came all the way from Heaven to say, 'Hi folks,' or whatever it was that he wanted to say.

There are many authentic cases where people have materialized back on Earth for some special reason, and, of course, if they want to be recognized, and that after all is the main reason for materializing, then they have to materialize in a pattern which is readily recognizable to the people who knew that person before his death. So always the person materializes as a very healthy specimen of the age group to which he belonged when he passed over. He always looks more beautiful than the Earth-child was, and that rejoices the parents' hearts.

If the parents really do love 'the child' they can meet in the astral, and first 'the child' appears as just that, as the identical child which died to Earth and was reborn to the astral. But as soon as the parents can recognize this, then the 'child' reappears as his natural self.

You must remember that although you have a mother and a father in this life they are not necessarily the same mother and father you will have in six hundred years time. You may have been the mother or the father, depending on your sex, of course, in a previous life. Actually people on Earth are just like a lot of actors coming to a stage; they take their clothes to suit the role they are going to play. So if an entity has to learn something as a woman it would be useless for that entity to come to Earth as a man, so instead she comes as a woman, and as a woman to a class which will enable her to learn those things which she came to learn.

'I wonder how it is that so many beings come to this world for the first time and encounter hunger, poverty, injustice, etc., when they don't have any previous debts and because kharmic justice shouldn't be negative for them.'

Well, they have to come somehow, haven't they? It is impossible for a person coming to Earth for the first time to come as a king or a queen. You can say they are 'new boys'. New boys at school, you know, the newest of new boys, most times have rather rough conditions, they are usually set upon by older boys and until they have 'worked their way in' they are not necessarily popular with the teachers either.

If one sets out as an apprentice one gets all the worst jobs to do, cleaning tools, cleaning equipment, sweeping floors and all the rest of it, and because they are only apprentices they do not have much money, they might even feel hungry on occasion. It doesn't mean that their kharma is at fault, because if they have just come to Earth for the first time, then they don't have much kharma, do they?

But we have to start somewhere. A person comes to the Earth-bound for the first time, and nearly always that person is a member of some savage race, some really savage tribe where he gets the rough corners knocked off and gets some training, no matter how rudimentary, of how humans go on.

It is unheard of for a person to come to, let us say, Europe or North America, as a first incarnation. He might come as a member of one of the savage backward tribes such as in Africa or Australia, one of those places where so-called civilization has hardly touched. Then he has to live according to the equipment he has, that is, is he a good natured person or is he nasty natured? If he is good natured then he will get on quite well. If he is unpleasant he wouldn't get on in any society at all. So, even in the very savage tribes a good natured person makes out better than a bad natured person.

Later the person incarnates into more and more advanced societies. By that time, of course, he has acquired a bit of kharma, not merely against him but also in his favour. So many have the utterly foolish notion that kharma is oppression, and it's not so at all. It's like a bank account. If you do a person good, then you have money in the bank. If you do a person some ill, then in effect you have lost money from the bank and so you are in debt. If you are in debt you have bad kharma. If you have money in the bank, then you have a credit balance and that credit is good kharma. If you have good kharma you can do things that you want to do and you can also trade on your good kharma so long as you do not do so much 'horse trading' that your good kharma or your credit balance disappears and you get into debt, because then you've got to work hard to get out of debt.

'It is said that we reincarnate many times but the time we stay in the astral plane varies according to the degree of evolution we have reached. The number of people will probably have to decline or be stabilized in the future, so what happens to all the souls who cannot come down to this material world to continue their reincarnation? Or will they have to remain in the astral for longer than their kharma really permits?'

But there again, you see, this talk about kharma. People do not have to reincarnate because of their kharma, they reincarnate because they want to learn something more. You don't necessarily go to college to pay somebody else, you go to college because you want to learn something. In just the same way you come to Earth because you want to learn something. If you wanted to pay off kharma, then you could pay off kharma by staying in the astral. There is a lot to be done there, and in doing good for others you do pay off kharma, but if you just stay in the astral – well, you remain 'as you were', and you are perhaps a drop-out from the school of Earth. If you want to progress more you come down to Earth and have some additional lessons in hardship, in tolerance, in patience and all that sort of thing. Get this quite clear, you do not come down to Earth just because someone else says you have to, you do not come down to Earth and have some suffering just because you have misbehaved yourself. You come to learn, and if conditions are a bit hard then it's no good blaming poor old kharma for it, it's what you choose yourself, it's the conditions you set up for yourself. Too many people take a rather peculiar satisfaction in saying, 'Oh, I couldn't help it, my kharma was against me.'

Of course there is kharma, but then of course there are

bank accounts. If you have something to sell or something which other people want, then you can get in money. If other people have something that you want, then you have to pay out for it and that means that you lose money. In the same way with kharma, if you do good to others then you are banking good kharma, but if you do ill to others then you are losing your good and getting a debit of bad kharma which has to be paid off sometime somewhere, not necessarily upon this Earth. Remember there are quite a lot of different worlds, and you will go to different worlds just as at school you had to go from class to class or grade to grade.

CHAPTER ELEVEN

A man has to hold his mouth
open a long time before a
roasted partridge flies into it.

THE Old Man snorted in the throes of pre-occupation, all these letters, all these questions, how to put within the compass of one book answers which would really help people, because that is the purpose of a book, isn't it? To help or to amuse. And this isn't an edition of comic cuts, it's meant to help, so let's get on with the first question.

'I am not at all clear on this kharma business. So everything we do affects someone else, does it? We must get an awful lot of kharma without knowing why we've got it.'

No, that is not true at all. People have the weirdest ideas about kharma, perhaps they haven't read my books properly. I sometimes get a letter from a person who writes so happily, 'Oh, Dr. Rampa, I read "Wisdom of the Ancients" last night, tonight I am going to read "Chapter of Life". I managed to go through "You – Forever" in two hours.' Well, of course that is just a waste of time, it doesn't do anyone any good, and it doesn't do an author any good to know that his books are being skimmed like that. These books are meant to be studied. Kharma is of vital importance to all of us, and in my books you have an opportunity of knowing what kharma is all about. It means, in brief, that if you do something wrong you pay for it. If you do something good, something pays you. As I have said before, it is like a bank account. You are like a storekeeper who has good and bad on the shelves. If you sell something that is good then you get paid by good, if you sell something that is bad you get paid by having an overdraft. Now get this quite clear;

whatever you do does not necessarily and automatically have an effect on any other person or creature. It depends entirely upon the circumstances. If, for example, you take a dagger and stick it into a person, then, of course, you are not doing a good deed, are you? In that case, then, you would have kharma against you. But if you do something which has an effect, a bad effect upon a person you have never heard of, an effect which you certainly did not anticipate, then you do not have to come back and pay off that person. I advise you, though, to read my books more thoroughly and then you will know a lot more about kharma.

Question: 'What are we doing down here, anyhow? When we leave here what is our objective, not just playing about in the astral, but what do we really want to do in the end?'

The Overself cannot of itself experience desire, suffering, pleasure, etc., *as we know it on Earth,* and so it is necessary for the Overself to have some other method of gaining knowledge. People upon Earth are just extensions of the Overself which can gain knowledge. For example, suppose you have a bag and you cannot get inside the bag and you cannot see inside the bag. If you can get it open enough to get your hand in, your hand, which is an extension of your other senses, can feel around inside the bag and can 'tell' the brain what there is inside. In much the same way the Overself gains information through the extensions called human beings.

When the Overself has sufficient knowledge, when the Overself is so advanced that no more knowledge on the Earth cycle is desired, then it calls home all the puppets which are humans, and they all merge again into the Overself, they become united in 'Oneness'; that is the ultimate form of existence because although it seems to be just one entity, each part of the entity lives in rapport with the other part. You have heard of twin souls – well, on the Earth plane it is impossible for twin souls to get together, but when they return to the Overself twin souls are reunited to form a perfect whole, and they live in a state of very great bliss until it occurs to the Overself that perhaps there is yet a higher form of knowledge which could be investigated. And then the Overself sends out puppets, not on the Earth plane, but on some super super plane, and the whole cycle is repeated. The puppets gather in the knowledge throughout a period which to us is eons of time. Again, when sufficient experience or knowledge has been garnered the Overself calls in the puppets, twin souls are again united in an even greater state of bliss.

Now here is a question from Miss Newman. She says, 'How should animals be destroyed so that death is painless and their astral body is not harmed?'

The best way is to inject some drug which causes the animal to lose consciousness, and then the method of disposing of the animal is not so important because there would be no pain. If an animal is made unconscious first, then it can be killed by some very rapid death-producing drug and that does not cause pain for the astral nor for the Overself. There is only distress to the astral when the physical is tormented by a slow killing.

Now here is something, this is a question from a young man whom we call 'Argie'. He will recognize himself. He is a remarkably brilliant young man who is his own worst enemy. He is a young man with truly unusual talents, and he is not using those talents to the best advantage because he wants to rebel against all authority. Argie has had a rough time, mostly of his own making. We will give two questions from Argie. The first:

'Genius in children; how does a child become a genius?'

In most cases the entity on the Other Side, before coming back to Earth, realizes that there is some special and specific task to do. It realizes that after a certain number of years it (the entity) may leave, and may perhaps leave a 'caretaker' in its place, so the entity makes plans whereby it comes down to Earth and is born into a body with a memory and an ability to do that which has to be done. For example, an entity may decide that something has to be done about a certain form of music, so it comes down with a memory of that almost intact. Then, just about as soon as it can speak or move of its own volition, the entity finds it can compose or play, and then it is said, 'We have a genius, we have an infant prodigy.' Most times the poor wretched child is stuck in front of a cine camera or something, or dumped on a stage to make money for people who do not know what it's all about, and the child is so busy making money that the inherited memory peters out.

In those cases where there are no stage shows and no cine shows the child may play divinely, and may compose exquisite music, and then when he reaches a certain age, let us say twenty years of age, the entity realizes that his task is done and he lets some other entity take over while he, the original occupant, moves on. This is called transmigration of souls, and it is far far more common than is generally supposed.

Argic has a second question, and here it is: 'Why do negroes rarely need tuition to play musical instruments?'

Negroes are a special type of people. Their basic vibrations are such that they are 'in tune to the music of the spheres'. Often a negro can hum music which he has never heard before, often he can just pick up a musical instrument and play it because that is his basic make-up.

You get certain classes of people such as North Europeans who are very cold and very analytical. They are very frigid in their attitude. That is their make-up. But if you get the Latin type of people they are warm in their make-up, quick to smile, quick to pass a joke. They can see the funny side of things – particularly if the misfortune happens to someone else. That is their make-up.

Negroes, for many years, have had a hard life, a life of persecution, and the only thing which has sustained them has been their musical make-up, their ability to derive consolation and solace from 'religious music'. As such it is part of their birthright, part of their heritage, part of their basic make-up. Negroes are usually very, very musical because their basic frequency is such that they sub-consciously pick up music from other sources in much of a way similar to the poor wretched man wearing a hearing aid who sometimes picks up transmissions from the local radio taxi cab company!

Well, let's get on with it; here is a question, 'I am a loving mother of a five year old boy, and your books, true as they are, scare me for what my son and all the other young children will have to suffer owing to events bigger than themselves. I can see him torn into pieces by atomic bombs and all grim pictures like those. His life lines on both his hands are abruptly interrupted at an age of about thirty to forty. I can find some consolation in your books for what concerns my death, but has ever a mother of any religion rejoiced at the death of her only son?'

Now, you are pre-supposing that your son will inevitably be killed or maimed in a forthcoming war, but remember that if you give him a good education and let him specialize in something he can be one of those protected. It is a sad thought that 'cannon fodder' is usually the person who is easily replaceable, whereas if a man is a specialist of use to his country he will be protected. So give your son a really good education. And in the matter of the hand lines, please be assured that if these are the only indications of the termination of his life, then they mean nothing except possibly a change of career. You should never take it as definite that death will occur unless there are about seven confirming indications. Too often palmists are guilty of criminal negligence in saying that a person is going to die, etc., etc., when it just means that they are going to change job and change location.

'You always state that death and after death are painless apart from the suffering at our own judgment, but in the Bardo Thodol and specifically in the Chonyd state the suffering seems to be atrocious.'

The Bardo Thodol was not written in English, it was just translated into that language by some creepish Christian who altered things a bit to make it tie in with the Christian belief of hellfire and damnation. There is no hellfire and damnation, that is all a misconception fostered by priests to bolster up their own power in much the same way as some misguided parents frighten their children by threatening to call in a policeman if they don't behave. Of course we are not happy when we are judging ourselves, it really does give us a pain when we see what stupid clods we have been. The self-contempt can be quite hellish, in fact, and well justify the description of 'hellfire'. As one who has total recall I tell you most emphatically that there is no torture, no atrocious pain, no ferocious suffering.

'Spirits who haunt old houses, have they not been reborn yet?'

Spirits who haunt old houses have nothing to do with current entities. For example, a person dies in tragic circumstances, and much energy is generated, but the person can go to a completely different plane and even be reborn while the energy which was generated will be dissipated in the form of hauntings. Its much the same as heating a piece of metal; the heat remains in the metal, although gradually fading, for quite a time after the source of heating has been removed. Here is a thought for you – it is quite possible for a person who dies in extremely difficult circumstances to have his energy as a thought form which haunts a place, and even to haunt the new-born incarnation who caused all the trouble in the first case?

'Are humans ever reborn as animals? The Bardo seems to be pretty incoherent in the matter, or may be I don't understand.'

No, humans are never reborn as animals, and animals are never reborn as humans. Nothing that you can do can turn a cabbage into a cow, nor can you change a rhinoceros into a rose, but I have dealt with this enough on preceding pages.

'What is nervous force, anyway? What's the good of telling us about nervous force if we have no idea what it is.'

Nervous force is the power which generates the etheric, and nervous force properly directed can rotate a paper cylinder, as I say in one of my books. Everybody, whether animal or human, is a generator of electricity, even the Earth has its magnetic force, its magnetic field if you prefer to call it that. And just as a radio programme has to have a carrier wave to support it, so does a human have to have an etheric consisting of nervous force or energy which propagates the aura. This in its turn originates from certain cells in the brain. The food we eat goes into the blood, and some of that food well mixed with oxygen goes to highly specialized brain cells, and provides the food for the generation of an electric current which powers the thought impulses. This is nervous force. If you find it difficult to believe, remember that you can get a device consisting of a zinc case with a few chemicals and a carbon rod inside it. If you connect that to a piece of wire inside a glass bulb from which air has been withdrawn you get a light, don't you, an electric light. So you get electricity from chemical reaction, and in the human you get electricity from chemical reaction provided by the food we eat.

I have a letter here from Mr. H. Mr. H. writes, 'I have enclosed two questions which you may care to answer. I would be very interested in the answer to question one, and would like to expand it a little. In addition to the matter of personal responsibility, which I think very important, I am confused on the matter of personal identity. This really boils down to the definition of the word "I". While I can see that in many ways "I" am not the same "I" that I was twenty years ago and presumably will not be the same as twenty years hence, yet I retain a sense of identity between these various I's.

'However, if an Overself can operate ten puppets what happens to the sense of "I", and when all puppets are dead does the Overself then continue to operate ten astral puppets, and continuing the thought into the future, what

happens if the ten puppets half succeed in liberating themselves?

'On a more particular note I have often wondered why it
was necessary for you to pick such an arduous route for your
journey to the West. Would it not have been possible for you
to go to a university in India or Europe, and could not funds
have been deposited in the West for your use? Many of your
troubles seem to have stemmed from a lack of money.'

Well, Mr. H., let's see what we can do to answer your
queries. Actually I think most of them have already been
answered in this book or in previous books, but let us write
you an imaginary letter.

'Dear Mr. H. You really are in a state of confusion, aren't
you? Much of your confusion arises from the fact that one
has to write in three dimensional terms and attempt to describe the operation of an Overself working, say, in a nine
dimensional plane of existence.

'You say that you think a puppet loses personal identity.
But of course, if you think about it, that is not the case.

'Look at that matter like this: Forget all about anything
outside the body, and assume for the purpose of this explanation that the body is "compartmental". The brain, then,
represents the Overself and everyone knows that the brain
directs the hands, the fingers, etc. The fingers represent
puppets and the brain can suggest that the fingers do something, but the fingers are still separate entities or separate
individuals, they can feel and they can become highy skilled.
In fact at times they seem to work of their own volition.

'The heart is another mechanism which cannot be controlled (except in abnormal cases) by the brain-Overself, because if the brain, representing our Overself, got in a bad
temper, then conceivably it could stop the heart from beating and that would destroy the entire mechanism of brain-
Overself and the organs-puppets. So, you see, the actual
Overself provides the substance from which the human
astrals are made, and each entity or human body has full
control and full choice of action always provided that such

action will not jeopardize the Overself-human organism.

'Take a big firm with many branches. There you have a chairman of the Board of Directors or a President. You have many departmental heads, and many general managers to staff all the district branches, and all these people work with their own responsibility while working within the framework of company policy. They do not have to tell the chairman of the Board of Directors every little thing, nor do they have to telephone him every moment about decisions which they are qualified to make.

'The chairman of the Board of Directors or the President, call him what you wish, represents the Overself, and all the departmental heads and managers are the puppets.

'You ask what happens when the puppets die, is the Overself, derived of its ten or so puppets, immobilized, you say. Let me ask you a question; what happens if one of the branch managers retires or is removed for some particular reason? The firm or branch does not close down. Instead a fresh manager, or puppet, is appointed. And anyhow in this chapter and possibly the chapter before I have already discussed how puppets return to the Overself.

'Yes, I could have taken an easy way. I could have gone to a university, I could have had sacks of gold all around me, but tell me, Mr. H., what sort of knowledge would I have gained then? I would be the reflection of other peoples' knowledge, some of it which is, admittedly, faulty. I would not have gained the knowledge of life which I have at present and which is very painfully firsthand, believe me. People who go to a University and learn everything the soft way merely learn the opinion of others from printed pages which may be years out of date. In a University a student may not dare to question the precepts of another. One is taught that it is impossible to do a thing except in the way specified in the text book, but the people who have not been to a University just go ahead and do the impossible thing anyway.

'Royce of Rolls-Royce, Edison, Ford, and thousands of

other very intelligent men did not go to a University, so they did not know that the thing which they wanted to do was "impossible", they did not know that such a thing was "impossible" because they lacked the education (!) to read the text books which really are the opinions of other people. And so Royce, Edison, Ford and others just went ahead and invented the things which text books would say were "impossible". So attendance at a university can be a drawback.

'That should straighten out a few questions for you, Mr. H., and I hope that you now find your thoughts are more settled.'

Another question asks why we have illness and how would it be possible to detect illness through the aura. Well, illness and disease come either from within or without. When it comes from without a germ or virus can be caught from another person and it is not the 'fault' of a body that catches it.

When we have a case of illness from within, that is, when the disease comes from within, the body chemicals are affected because everything comes from thought, what the electricians call electro-motive force comes into play. Thought is electric impulses. When we think we generate electricity. The electricity is thus the electro-motive force which causes our muscles to work, or even upsets our body chemistry. If a person is frustrated, worried, sad, bad tempered, etc., or has an abnormal emotion, their thoughts generate an electric current which is defective. It may not have the necessary correct wave form, and because the electric current is defective it causes wrong messages to go to the glands and the glands' secretion change to cope with the wrong thoughts and the wrong messages caused by those wrong thoughts. After a time the most susceptible part is affected by the changed secretions, or changed chemical balance of the body. It may be the muscles that are affected, and so one gets, perhaps, muscular dystrophy, or it might be something to do with the bones, it might be arthritis, or, if some wrong message causes a disturbance in the stomach, the gastric juices may become too acid, too strong, and then we might have an ulcer. Closer to home, if the messages are too localized and affect the brain, then there might be a brain tumor.

If the chemistry can be studied then it can be corrected by hormone treatment or some other appropriate treatment and the disease can be cured if it is caught in time. If too much damage has been done, then it can't be cured but can be alleviated. The person should remedy the thing or emotion that caused the damage in the first place by getting a more balanced outlook, by controlling the emotions, or by a changed set of circumstances such as fresh job, fresh partner, etc.

All these things can be seen in the aura. Whatever happens to a body can be seen in the aura. Looking at the aura is like looking at radar pictures. You can see land or a storm disturbance which is quite beyond ordinary sight.

Whether an illness starts from 'within' or 'without' it can be detected from the aura. If one catches an infection from some other person then it takes a certain time for that illness to manifest substantially in the physical, yet in the aura at the exact instant when the infection took place it shows quite clearly, it shows like lines of stress.

If the illness is caused from 'within' then a periodical examination of the aura will show the danger of an illness quite a long time before the body is seriously affected, and so the illness can be cured almost before it has become apparent.

In connection with this, I have been working on such a matter for a whole lifetime and the biggest difficulty has been getting people to part with their clothes. There was a certain noble lady in England with whom I was discussing the matter. We were only talking about it, and this very noble lady, who had been married and has a family of her own, said, 'Oh! You want nude bodies. Most definitely I should do everything to oppose anything which required a woman to remove her clothing or to expose certain portions of her body.' I, with great restraint, refrained from reminding the noble lady that even she had to expose a certain portion of her body so that her babies could be born.

CHAPTER TWELVE

If you don't believe in others
how can you expect others to
believe in you.

THE Old Man lay back on his bed. The evening sun was just setting behind the low hills sending its last rays gleaming on the placid water of the Saint John River.

Off to the left the paper factory was still belching out furious clouds of smoke and steam as it did twenty-fours a day, obscuring the sky and polluting the atmosphere. Into the river poured all the waste products making an incredible stench in the air of Saint John, a stench about which everyone complained, and about which no one did anything.

The snows were melting fast. This was spring, the start of spring, but now with the fast setting sun dipping behind the hills birds were scurrying along in droves hurrying to get home to their perches while the light yet held.

Directly below the window Sinjin, a telepathic cat, was singing a lonely song, inviting all the cat ladies of the neighbourhood to come and be welcomed by him. His voice rose and fell, quavering with the intensity of his emotion. From time to time he stopped, raised his head high, and even sat upright on his back legs like a rabbit while he listened intently for any calls that his invitation was being accepted. Disappointed that he had no such intimation, he dropped to all fours again and with his tail twitching with emotion he started all over again like an old-time London costermonger, crying his wares, but nothing of 'any old iron, any old rags'; this was a different cry: 'love for free, come quick, I'm waiting'.

Cars drove up with a roar and a clatter and store keepers and their assistants drove into the parking lot with much elan and got out of their cars with great slamming of doors and calling of 'Goodnight – goodnight', before hurrying up the steps in the constant fight to get room in the elevator.

The Old Man lay back and thought of the past, thought of the difficulties of this life, thought of the few, few pleasures and the many, many hardships. A hard life, yes, he thought. But, praise be, the last time on this round, the last time on this Earth. And now, he thought, I have just about cleared up all that has to be done, cleared up all those empty corners, turned out the attics, even tossed out the garbage.

'Not so, not so,' said a most familiar and well-loved voice. 'The task is not yet ended, you have done more than you came to do, but – the task is not yet ended.'

The Old Man turned on his side and there right close to him was the super-astral figure of the Lama Mingyar Dondup, smiling and with a brilliant gold radiance. 'You quite startled me,' said the Old Man, 'and I wish you'd turn your lights low, it reminds me of when I was in England, in London.'

'Oh, what was that?' asked the Lama Mingyar Dondup. 'Is it something which I do not know?'

'I think it must be,' said the Old Man, 'let me tell you about it. I was in a building in South Kensington late at night, and I was sitting in the dark thinking, just thinking over things, just meditating, and for some reason I had not pulled the blinds. Suddenly there came a tremendous knocking at the door down below. I started back to awareness and went down to see what was the cause of the commotion. Two big beefy London bobbies were there. 'Sir,' said one – a sergeant I saw by his stripes – 'what are you doing in this building?' 'Doing?' I replied. 'I don't think I was doing anything. I was just sitting thinking as a matter of fact.' 'Well,' replied the Sergeant, 'we were called here in a great hurry

185

because you were shining very bright lights out of the window.' 'Oh,' I replied, 'I most certainly was not, but if I had been is that a crime?'

'The sergeant looked at his subordinate, and shrugging his shoulders said, "Well, it might be, you know. You might be signalling to a crime gang to show that the road is clear or something." Then he came to a decision. "I want to search the place." I said, "have you a search warrant?" "No," he replied, "but if you do not give me permission to search the place I can leave the constable here to watch you while I go and get the necessary warrant."

'So I just shrugged my shoulders and said, "All right, go where you like, look where you like." So the two policemen wandered around, looked at everything, and most extraordinary of all, they pulled out the drawers of my desk and looked inside. I don't know what they thought they would find there. But anyway, after about three quarters of an hour they appeared satisfied, and as they were leaving the sergeant said, "Don't do it again, sir, please. It makes too much work." And off they went.'

The Lama Mingyar Dondup laughed, 'Whatever you do, Lobsang,' he said, 'you seem to attract the wrong sort of attention. I can't think of anyone else who would be almost arrested just for showing his aura when he was thinking.'

The Old Man was looking a bit gloomy as he said, 'So you think my task is not finished, eh? What haven't I done now?'

The Lama Mingyar Dondup replied, 'You've done everything. It's not a question that you have left anything undone. You have done more, much more than you came here to do, but it so happens that through the failure of others there is still more to do.'

'What?' asked the Old Man.

The Lama Mingyar Dondup looked down his nose and tried not to smile as he said, 'There may be another book to make the twelfth. We shall have to think about it. It would certainly be appreciated. But there is another little task which has to be done, something in connection with an invention which may yet burst upon this startled world.'

For some time the Old Man and the Lama Mingyar Dondup discussed things, but this is not the place to disclose all that was said. The Old Man, sick almost to death, and with expenses mounting through medical bills, and other vital expenditures, wondered how he was going to stick it for even a few months longer. At last the super-astral of the Lama Mingyar Dondup faded, and the failing daylight took over once again.

Time. What a strange thing is this artificial time. One could travel from the astral world here and back in the twinkling of an eye, and yet down here on this Earth one was bound by the clock and by the motion of the sun controlling the clock. Here in New Brunswick the sun was setting. A few thousand miles away John Henderson would still be busy at his work about in the middle of the afternoon. Not so far away Valeria Sorock, that paragon of loyalty and exactitude, would probably just be leaving her office and probably thinking of her tea. Yes, most certainly, thought the Old Man, Valeria would be thinking of her tea because one weakness was that she thought too much of food! 'I shall have to talk to her about her diet,' thought the Old Man to himself.

In the other direction the Worstmann ladies would probably be at home very late in the evening, perhaps listening to the radio, perhaps studying, and perhaps one of them just about to go on night duty.

But here the ladies Taddy and Cleo were having their evening play, chasing around with a favourite toy, and the favourite toy was a nice, soft, woolly belt from a dressing gown. The Old Man thought of Taddy and Cleo, thought of how since they were born they had been treated as human children, how everything had been done to make them feel that they were entities as important as any humans, and the task had been most frutiful, the results had been most gratifying, for these two little people were indeed real people.

From midnight until midday Miss Cleo was mentioned first, but from midday until midnight Miss Taddy's name was mentioned first and so they were assured of quite equal treatment without any trace of favouritism.

Miss Taddy, ample, plump, and comfortable looking, loves to crouch down behind one of the scratch pads while the extremely beautiful, very slender, very graceful Miss Cleo bounces up and down and does wildly improbable feline gymnastics.

But the night was growing darker, the air was growing colder and there still was a nip of frost about. Outside the red of the thermometer was dropping, outside people on the road were well muffled up.

The Old Man had been looking forward to this day, the day when the eleventh book would be ended and he could push aside all thoughts of writing and say, 'Never any more, it's all over, no more writing, my time on Earth has just about finished.' But now with the visit from the super-astral of the Lama Mingyar Dondup – well, the Old Man thought, isn't one's task ever ended, is one driven along like a rickety old car until it finally falls to pieces? I'm just about in pieces now, he thought. But there it is, what will be will be, and when a task has to be done, it will not be done unless there is someone there to do it. So, thought the Old Man, I must try to hang on a little longer, and as for writing another book, who knows? It might be good to make the number in English up to twelve. He thought, 'I would like to tell everyone, everyone throughout the world, that all these books are true, everything related in these books is true, and that is a definite statement.'

So we come to the end of what is not a perfect day after all because the task is not ended, the final battle is not yet won, there is more to be done, and little time and little health with which to do it. We can but try.

Here and now let me offer my most grateful thanks to Mrs. Sheelagh Rouse, alias Buttercup, for the immense care and work she has devoted to typing my books, care and work which is appreciated perhaps more than she knows.

Let me offer my thanks to Ra'ab for the extreme care and accuracy with which she has checked everything and made truly worthwhile suggestions. She has aided my task.

And finally, but by no means least, let me thank Miss Tadalinka and Miss Cleopatra Rampa for the encouragement and entertainment they have given to me. These two dear little people have made it worthwhile to continue a little longer for never in the whole of their four years of life have they shown any spite, any bad temper, and not even any irritation. If humans were as equable and sweet-natured as these two there would be no trouble on the Earth, no wars. Then it would indeed be the Golden Age for which people must yet wait.

And so at last we come, in this book, to the time when we can say 'The End'.

OTHER BOOKS BY T. LOBSANG RAMPA

THE HERMIT

The cave which just moments before had been pitch black was now filled with excessive light and suddenly the the old hermit—who had been blind for countless years—could see. Before him stood The Wise Ones—majestic beings with brilliant auras, perfect in nearly every way. Escorted into their bizarre (to him, anyway) craft, the Hermit was flown into space. Before him on a giant screen were flashed scenes of the seeding of Earth by the Creators; a fierce battle in the depths of space between Satan and God's Forces; the truth about all religions; the years Christ spent in Tibet; the Great Flood; the arrival of the Gardeners (their history goes back millions of years) from space, and much, much more. This book is packed with sacred truths as can only be related by T. Lobsang Rampa.—**$12.95**

Available March 1991

FEEDING THE FLAME

As the author lay desperately ill in a hospital, he looked up with pleasure to see his old friend and mentor, the Lama Mingyar Donup, standing by his bedside. But it was with some dismay that he listened to the message that the Golden Figure had brought. Rampa's work on this plane was not, as he thought, completed…he was told that he could not as yet pass on to the next plane, but that he had more mystic truths to reveal to the world. Here is Rampa's observations on such intriguing subjects as Life After Death, Suicide, Meditation, Ouija Boards, Demons, the Astral Body, Organ Transplants, etc.—**$12.95**

Available Now by
special arrangement with
Samuel Weiser, Inc.

YOU FOREVER

Thirty metaphysical lessons designed for the reader to work at their own pace. Step-by-step methods for seeing the human aura, traveling in the astral plane. Learn to see clairvoyantly. Written in Rampa's usual warm, humorous and charming manner. A full 288 pages.—**$12.95**

Available from your local book seller or from mail order. Add $1 to total order for 4th class book rate or $2.50 for UPS shipping and send to:

INNER LIGHT PUBLICATIONS
Box 753, New Brunswick, NJ 08903

NJ residents add sales tax. Allow 4–6 weeks for delivery

INNER LIGHT PUBLICATIONS
BOX 753
NEW BRUNSWICK, N.J. 08903